PROCLAIMING
HIS
KINGDOM

PROCLAIMING HIS KINGDOM

JOHN FUELLENBACH, SVD

Second Edition

DIVINE WORD PUBLICATIONS
Manila

First Edition, 1988

The **Society of the Divine Word (SVD)** is an international missionary congregation of priests and brothers serving in more than fifty countries all over the world. Through the Divine Word Publications, the SVD in the Philippines aims to foster the apostolate of the printed word in the theological, catechetical and pastoral fields in order to promote justice, peace and human development as revealed by the Divine Word made flesh. The opinions expressed by the authors do not necessarily reflect those of the SVD community.

Copyright © 1992 Society of the Divine Word
Published by **LOGOS Publications, Inc.**
All Rights Reserved
Manufactured in the Republic of the Philippines

Cover Design: **LEONILO T. HERNANDEZ**
Cover Illustration: **JOSE WINSTON T. HERNANDEZ**

ISBN: 971-510-065-1

TABLE OF CONTENTS

PREFACE
TO THE SECOND EDITION.

Since the earlier editions of this small volume was so well received, the basic content of this revised edition will remain the same. The new text is stylistically reworked and necessary corrections were made by Fr. Patrick Connor, SVD to whom I owe a special word of thanks. A number of new stories are added or replaced, and the questions for reflection are partly reworded. Two new conferences were added: **Conversion of St. Paul** and **Poverty: Option for the Poor.**

Special thanks goes to Sister Christel Daun, S.Sp.S. for her help in selecting the stories, and helping in so many ways with the new edition.

We had some difficulty earlier selecting a suitable title. Although the book was originally meant for religious and priests, it surprisingly reached many lay people as well who want to follow the Lord more dedicatedly. We, therefore, decided to leave the title as it was worded in the second printing.

Rome, Pentecost 1992

Fr. John Füllenbach, SVD

FOREWORD

The Kingdom of God has always fascinated me. Over the past twenty years, I have been teaching this vision of Jesus to seminarians, sisters, priests and lay people in many different countries. It never fails to stir up the imagination of people of all ages, races and cultures.

On the basis of the Kingdom, I have worked out a retreat which I have given to priests, seminarians, sisters and lay people. I have preached this retreat more than two hundred times in various situations and countries of the world.

I have now decided, at the urgings of friends and those who gained most from this retreat, to put it down in writing.

The retreat is a witness to my own faith, as the many little stories prove. To publish such personal experiences is to give away something of one's self and one normally hesitates to do this. However, since it is meant to be a witness to the Kingdom present among us, I will gladly share what I myself have received without the merits of my own.

Most of the thoughts presented here are based on my own personal experiences as a priest, missionary, seminary professor and counsellor to so many people. I owe a debt of gratitude to Sister Therese Ryder who helped me in so many ways to prepare these pages and to Fr. John Musinsky, a confrere with whom I worked together in so many retreats, recollections and workshops. Some ideas I even "stole" from him.

My only wish is that those who read these pages may come to experience for themselves the unconditional love of God and find in this love the strength and the joy necessary to continue to witness to Christ and his Kingdom with renewed enthusiasm and zeal.

I dedicate this work to my parents whose deep faith and love for the Lord were the "outstretched finger" which directed me to Christ and made it all possible for me.

Fr. John Fuellenbach, SVD
Nemi, Italy

AIM AND PURPOSE OF A RETREAT

"My soul thirsts for you, O Lord."

A retreat is a time to pray, to meditate, to reflect but primarily it is a time to listen more intensely to the Lord living in me. What is he trying to say to me? Do I want to know what areas in my life need to be changed and which ones need healing? And if I should come to see them, do I really want them to be changed and healed? In John 5:6 Jesus asks the lame man: "Do you want to be healed?" The question as directed to me would mean: Do I really want the Lord to heal me knowing what consequences it would have in my life in the way I live and behave. Do I really want to be changed and to live a life different from the one I have known up to now?

During a retreat I might have to wrestle with the Lord as Jacob did and go away limping - a constant reminder that God is the stronger one. In Genesis 32:23-32 Jacob received the name Israel, which means: God will prevail. God was the one who prevailed over all Jacob's evasive behavior towards Him. He was the stronger one. God won in the life of Jacob. So I ask: Is God the one who prevails over my life and to what degree? Or, I might have to look even more seriously at my life as this text of Revelation indicates:

> I know all about you; how you are reputed to be alive and yet are dead. Wake up; revive what little you have left; it is dying fast. So far I have failed to notice anything in the way you live that my God could possibly call perfect, and yet do you remember how eager you were when you first heard the message? Hold on to that. Repent (Rv 3:1-3).

Presuppositions for a good retreat

A good retreat presupposes a few things, like:

1. A hunger and thirst for God

"I am the bread of life," Jesus told them. "He who comes to me will never be hungry; he who believes in me will never be thirsty" (Jn 6:35).

As a doe longs for running waters so my soul thirst for God, the God of my life. When shall I go and see the face of God? (Ps 43:1-2).

Without such a hunger it will be difficult if not almost impossible for me to hear the voice of God, to get in touch with him or be reassured of his presence in my life.

How great is this hunger and thirst for God in me now?

There was a young man who approached a hermit with this request: "Show me how I can find God." "How great is this desire of yours?" asked the saintly man. "More than anything in the world," came the reply. The hermit took the young man to the shore of a lake and they waded into the water until it was up to their necks. Then the holy man put his hand on the other's head and pushed him under water. The young man struggled desperately, but the hermit did not release him until he was about to drown. When they returned to the shore, the saint asked, "Son, when you were under water, what did you want more than anything in the world?" "Air," he replied without hesitation. "Well, then, when you want to find God as much as you just then wanted air, your eyes will be opened to the wonder of God." (P.J. Wharton, *Stories and Parables*)

2. The Help of the Holy Spirit

Without him we can do nothing. A constant cry to him for enlightenment, strength and guidance should accompany every day of the retreat. Our helplessness without him is indicated by these passages from Scripture:

And Yahweh said, "I am going to speak to you." As he said these words the spirit came into me and made me stand up, and I heard him speaking to me (Ez 2:1).

I fell flat on my face downward on the ground. Then I heard a voice saying, "Mortal man, stand up, I want to talk to you. While the voice was speaking God's Spirit entered me and raised me to my feet and I heard his voice.

I saw a hand reaching out towards me, and it was holding a scroll. The hand unrolled the scroll...God said, "Mortal man, eat this scroll; then go and speak.." I opened my mouth, and he gave me the scroll to eat. He said, "Eat this scroll that I give you; fill your stomach with it." I ate it and it tasted as sweet as honey (Ez 2:9-3:3).

The Spirit comes to help us, weak as we are. For we do not know how we ought to pray; the Spirit himself pleads with God for us in groans that words cannot express (Rm 8:26).

There are things we do not know: we do not know how to make a successful retreat; neither does a retreat-master know how to give a retreat, because only the Spirit can touch the hearts of the participants. The retreat-master can bring God's word to the ears of his listeners, but it is the Holy Spirit who alone can bring it from the ear into the heart. Only he can make it become effective in the lives of the participants.

Only when the Spirit speaks in us and is present in us can we really make a good retreat.

WITHOUT THE HOLY SPIRIT: God is far away, Christ stays in the past, the Gospel is a dead letter, the Church is simply an organization, authority is a matter of domination, mission a matter of propaganda, the liturgy no more than an evocation, Christian living a slave morality.

WITH THE HOLY SPIRIT: the cosmos is resurrected and groans with the birth pangs of the Kingdom, the risen Christ is there, the Gospel is the power of life, the Church shows forth the life of the Trinity, authority is a liberating service, mission is a Pentecost, the liturgy is both memorial and anticipation, human action is deified. (From a Pentecost homily given by Patriarch Athenagoras)

3. Prayer

In the seminary we had a famous professor who would tell us: "Always remember when you give a retreat, the only part of a retreat that remains, no matter how good the retreat-master might be, is the hours your retreatants have spent in prayer with the Lord. The rest they will most probably forget."

But what should I pray for? The prayer St. Paul prays for his co-workers and his communities seems to be the best.

I pray that Christ will be more and more at home in your heart, living within you as you trust him. May your roots go down deep into the soil of God's marvelous love and may you be able to feel and understand, as all God's children should, how long, how wide, how deep and high his love really is; and experience his love for yourselves (Ep 3:17-19).

Let your roots grow down into him and draw nourishment from him. See that you go on growing in the Lord and become strong and vigorous in the truth you were taught (Col 2:7).

Theme of our retreat: Fellowship With the Lord

It is a good idea to give a theme to a retreat in order to indicate the direction it will take. I propose to call it: OUR WAY OF FOLLOWING AND IMITATING THE LORD. There is only one vocation for all who call themselves Christians. It is the most essential of them all, whether we are lay-people, religious, priests, bishops or even the pope, namely: THE CALL TO FOLLOW THE LORD. But this one vocation for all knows different ways, different styles of life. There is the way of following the Lord as a family man or woman. There is the priestly way of following the Lord and the religious way of contemplative and active life. The Second Vatican Council describes the way of religious and priests as that of "following the Lord MORE freely and imitating him MORE nearly" as he presents himself in the Gospel (*Perfectae Caritatis* 1).

The religious and priestly way of following the Lord is marked by a radicalism which Paul expresses in this way:

I reckon everything as complete loss for the sake of what is so much more valuable, the knowledge of Christ Jesus my Lord. For his sake I have thrown everything away. I consider it all as mere garbage, so that I might gain Christ and be completely united with him (Ph 3:8-9).

A retreat, from this point of view, is a time to examine oneself in the light of this declaration of St. Paul. What does Christ really mean to me? Is he priority number one in my life? Does he rule my life?

Many people, including theologians and spiritual writers, are concerned about the meaningfulness and relevance of our Christian faith and ask the question: How can we present the Christian message today to people who live in a socio-cultural and political environment different from that of Christ's time? In the 'developed world' we face the challenge of a totally secularized society. In Latin America and Africa the non-person who is oppressed and exploited looks at his/her traditional faith and asks: Does it have anything to say to our situation that could help us to overcome it? In Asia the great religious traditions which are older than Christianity look at us and ask: what can your faith give us that we do not yet have?

I don't have the answer to these questions but something becomes clearer every day. Some years ago the German Bishops' Conference framed their solution in these words: "The way out of the crisis in which we find ourselves today can only be a way into fellowship with the Lord." The important words are: the WAY OUT can only be a WAY INTO following the Lord.

There are times in the history of our faith and in our lives when we have to admit our utter helplessness and humbly go back to the Lord and start walking behind him once again as the first disciples did and try to put our feet into his footprints. Like Peter we are asked to walk behind the Lord and not to pretend to know which way the Lord wants us to walk (Mk 8:29-33). At such times we may be asked to do what Peter was told to do: to "let himself be led where he would rather not go" (Jn 21:18).

There are two basic questions which we will have to ask ourselves in this retreat: How far is following the Lord the prime priority in my life? What precisely does it mean to follow the Lord in my state of life today?

Am I willing to walk behind the Lord and let him determine the way? In the Old as well as in the New Testament discipleship literally means: to go behind the Master and let him lead the way. It means to put one's shoes into the footprints of the one who goes ahead. In Mark 8:33 it is as though Jesus is saying: "Peter, get behind me and put your shoes into my footprints and don't tell me which way to walk if you want to be a disciple of mine."

Our Vocation as a Personal Relationship

My Christian vocation is a profession I have to practice, or a job I have to do eight hours a day after which I go home, be myself, relax and start living. No, my vocation is a way of life, a personal relationship with someone. Therefore, it means I have to take time out to be with that person. I will have to WASTE a lot of time with him if I really want our relationship to remain sound and grow ever deeper. Friendship is like a path. If it is not walked on regularly it will soon be overgrown with all kinds of weeds and thorns. A personal relationship with someone asks for time, lots of time. It requires being with the person often without saying anything, just being present. This alone is the atmosphere in which friendship, intimacy and true love can grow. The time we spend with someone helps us to see that person as precious. It is the time you spend in prayer with the Lord that will make this retreat a good one. Prayer, according to Teresa of Avila, means: "To be with him whom we know loves us."

It is important to regard the time of a retreat as a special gift from the Lord, an opportunity which he offers you, an invitation to grow in and to experience his friendship for you. You can waste this opportunity, but remember that there are times when the doors of welcome are wider open.

> Right now God is ready to welcome you. Today he is ready to save you (2 Cor 6:2).

> Harden not your heart this day, if you hear his voice (Psalm 95).

> God is always enjoying us. He is always looking at us with love. Christian contemplation dares to admit to the possibility that Jesus is contemplating me at every moment. That he knows me and loves me. (E.Farrell, *Free to be Nothing*)

The Lord is Seeking You and Not You Seeking Him

It is important to realize that during a retreat it is not you who is seeking the Lord. It is the Lord who is seeking you. Read once again the beautiful story about God and us portrayed in the image of an unfaithful woman and a husband who is hopelessly in love with her in spite of her unfaithfulness (Hosea 2:1-16). God's love cannot let her go; his heart is sick with love. So too God runs after each one of us all the time. His call is: "Adam, where are you?" God wants to talk with you during these days. Be at home and search for him in your own heart.

> The fact is, however, that if you descend into the depths of your spirit... and arrive somewhere near the center of what you are, you are confronted with the inescapable truth that, at the very root of your existence, you are in constant and immediate and inescapable contact with the infinite power of God. (T. Merton, *The Contemplative Life*)

> Unless we discover this deep self, which is hidden with Christ in God we will never really know ourselves as persons. Nor will we know God. For it is by the door of this deep self that we enter into the spiritual knowledge of God. (T. Merton, *The New Man*)

> And look, all the time you were inside of me at the middle and I was outside of myself, on the margin. You were with me, and I was not with you (and hence not with myself) and I was going to pieces in the beautiful things you yourself had made. (Augustine, *Confessions*)

The means for entering within are very simple, because to meditate means doing two things:

To consider - to dwell on something thoughtfully, to open yourself in silence to **a hidden mystery,** the experience of his presence in you now. What is this mystery in us to which we should open ourselves in silence? St. Paul puts it this way:

The secret is this: **Christ in you,** the hope of a glory to come (Col 1:24-27).

Meditation and prayer as human activities mean simply "to make myself present to the presence of Christ within me." Or, "to search for my 'hidden self' in me and to let it grow strong."

To execise perseveringly - to return again and again to something with love and to develop it. Only in this way will I come to realize his presence in me and start living this mystery in all my relationships with persons and things. In the words of St. Paul:

Put yourselves to the test and judge yourselves, to find out whether you are living in faith. Surely you know that **CHRIST JESUS LIVES IN YOU?** (2 Cor 13:5).

What Can I Realisitically Expect From This Retreat?

After having made so many retreats you might be tempted to say with the prophet: "Lord can these dry bones still live?" (Ez 37:1-14) Or with Nicodemus you might ask the Lord: "How can a grown person be born again?" Jesus answers Nicodemus: "The wind (Spirit) blows wherever it wishes" (Jn 3:2-12).

Another beautiful Bible story to this point is Elijah's encounter with the Lord which images so many of us. Elijah had gone into a cave to escape from his persecutors. Yahweh comes and asks him, "What are you doing here, Elijah?" He answers, "They are after my life." "Go out of your cave and stand at the entrance and wait for Yahweh", he is told. Then Yahweh himself passes by. But he is not in the mighty wind; he is not in the earthquake; he is not in the fire. These are all means through which people thought Yahweh would make his presence known. After the fire, comes the sound of a gentle breeze. And when Elijah heard this he covered his face with his cloak and went out and stood at the entrance of the cave. Then a voice spoke within him saying, "What are you doing here, Elijah?" (1Kg 19:9-15)

The answer, then, to the question: What can you expect in this retreat is: To hear God's voice in the gentle breeze. Don't expect God to make himself known to you in only traditional ways. Elijah met God in that dark and quiet place within. He heard his voice in himself: "What are you doing here Elijah?" Elijah managed to get out of the dark cave and stand at its entrance. He is finally ready to hear God's word. God tries his question once again, helping his prophet to bring into the open the state of his soul and to see his need for conversion.

> I have given retreats of many different kinds. I remember once giving a directed retreat to a Brother who was a simple man and a mechanic by trade. Since this was his first directed retreat, I asked him at its conclusion, "What did you discover in this retreat?" His answer was concise and came without any hesitation, almost as if he had expected my question, "I discovered two things which I never knew before. Firstly, I can be a man of prayer. That is something I never thought possible. I really can pray two, three hours a day if I want. Secondly, every page of the Bible speaks to me personally. Scripture is really a word of God to me."

I have learnt over the years that Scripture is the most powerful means to achieve change in one's life. The word of God is something that is alive and can touch human hearts (Heb 4:12).

Gregory the Great once said, "God directs his words to you, learn to discover his heart in them." Sacred Scripture can also prove to you that it is a store from which the householder can produce "things old and new" (Mt 13:52).

However, to have a sense or feeling for God's heart, one has to be touched. Let the Lord touch you in the way Michelangelo has portrayed it so beautifully in his picture of the creation of Adam. May what happened to St. Augustine happen to you, in these days, "Lord, you have touched me and now I burn."

If you realize that it is not you but God who accomplishes great things in your life, then you can expect great things also in this retreat. What you can expect is beautifully expressed in this modern version of Psalm 40 by Leslie F. Brandt:

> I searched long and shouted loud for God.
> It finally paid off, and He responded.
> He reached into my pathetic emptiness
> and planted objective and purpose there.
> Now I feel like singing;
> there is genuine meaning for my life.
> And maybe I can sell others on this concept
> of really finding themselves in God...
> There is love and concern there,

and meaning and purpose,
far more than one can possibly imagine...

It was when I turned from self-seeking
to embrace His will for my life
that I discovered serenity and security.

All this, however, does not mean that you will be able to solve all your problems in this retreat. None of us solves his or her own problems, either directly or indirectly. Rather, God inclines me in the right direction. He sheds light on my problems in the total context of my calling. My role is to be open to him in prayer in order to get to know who I am, willing to face the truth about myself and to accept changes wherever they are necessary. In short, I am being invited to let God do for me the things he wants to do.

Questions for Reflection:

1.Is there a real hunger for God in my life?

2.Do I want the Lord to heal me from my blindness, lameness and paralysis knowing what consequences it would have in my life?

3.How far is following the Lord really the prime priority in my life?

4.Am I willing to enter the 'dark and quiet place within' - and then 'stand at the entrance to hear God's word?'

Story for Reflection:

FOR WHOM DO YOU WALK?

In a village in Russia in the last century, the rich people protected their property by hiring people who would watch over it during the night. One evening Rabbi Naftalis was walking at the edge of one of these properties and he ran into one of the watchmen who was making his rounds. The Rabbi asked him, "For whom are you walking, young man?" The watchman told him the name of the owner but he added, "And you, Rabbi, for whom are you walking?" The word hit the Rabbi like a flying arrow. After a long silence with some effort he replied, "At the moment I am not walking for anyone." Then the Rabbi asked, "Are you willing to become my servant?" Of course, with pleasure, the watchman replied, "but what will I have to do?" The Rabbi answered, "You will have to remind me for whom I am supposed to walk." *(Chassidic Tradition)*

For whom do you walk? In whose service are you living?

CONVERSION: A CONSTANT DEMAND OF THE KINGDOM PRESENT AMONG US

Introduction

The theme of our retreat is: OUR WAY OF FOLLOWING THE LORD. Fellowship with the Lord is our essential vocation. That means, to make Jesus' cause my cause, his concern my concern, his convictions my convictions, his ideas my ideas and his world view my world view, in short, to make his vision my vision.

The criterion as to whether or not your life will be a success in view of your vocation depends not on what you have achieved, accomplished or built up in this world but ultimately on how you responded to that simple invitation of the Lord, "Come, follow me."

God will not ask you how successful you have been in this life but how faithful you have been in your following the Lord. Following the Lord however means to make Jesus' vision my own and to let it determine my whole life. But what precisely is Jesus' cause, his concern, his world-view, his vision that I have to make my own? Jesus compared it with fire. "I came to throw fire into this world and how much do I desire to see it burning" (Lk 12:49). For this vision he lived, labored, suffered and died. Since Jesus came, the Kingdom of God is at hand. It is a reality that is constantly breaking into this world, surrounding us all the time.

The correct image of God

In what does this vision consist? It is the correct image of God. Jesus came to disclose to us the true image of God. He came to correct our false concepts of God by showing us a new way of thinking about God. His is the only way to think about God correctly:

> No one has ever seen God, it is the only Son, who is nearest to the Father's heart who has made him known (Jn 1:18).

The infantile and erroneous images that many people have about God are mind-boggling and sad. God for them is some one who is angry, who is out to "get" them; he is a God who makes people feel guilty and worthless. These images are the demons that Jesus came to expel. Jesus teaches us three important lessons: God always loves us, God always forgives us, God is always present with us.

What image of God do you have? Karl Rahner once said, "The way we know, love, treasure the things presented to us is the way we know and love God." And it is equally true to say that the actual knowledge and personal experience of "who God is for me in my daily life" ultimately determines how I see, love and treasure the things presented to me. In short, one could say, "Tell me how you experience God and who he is for you, and I will tell you how you relate to and evaluate your environment."

> Psychologists tell us, we are related to four environments: to ourselves, to friends and family, to institutions and society (race, nation, church, world, etc.) and lastly, to nature and climate. We are somehow the sum total of our experiences, the complex of our relationship with ourselves, with others, with society and with the universe. (John Shea, *Stories of God*)

How do I treasure these elements of my environment? This depends ultimately on my image of God. But that is exactly what revelation is all about and what Christ came to reveal to us, namely, who God really is and what we are meant to be.

What kind of God did Jesus reveal?

Jesus revealed his image of God not in abstract terms and theological definitions but in parables and symbolic actions. The most vivid ones are probably found in Luke chapter 15. A. Greeley once remarked, "If we would have nothing of what Jesus said and did, except the three stories of Luke 15 - the Prodigal Son, the Lost Sheep and the Lost Coin - we would still have the essence of his message."

Others have singled out the following three parables that demonstrate most clearly the image of God that Jesus came to reveal. The Laborers in the vineyard or the Parable of the Good Employer (Mt 20:1-16); The Parable of the Unmerciful Servant or the Parable of the Merciful Master (Mt 18:21-35); The Parable of the Prodigal Son or the Parable of the Unbelievably Merciful Father (Lk 15:11-32).

What is the outstanding message of these parables? They reveal the true image of God that Jesus came to communicate to us: a God whose basis for dealing with us is unbelievable, compassionate love. The behavior in all three parables is the most unlikely that a reasonable human being would take. This is precisely the point Jesus wants to make in these parables: God is someone who acts out of love and not out of rationality or even common sense. Like any true lover God behaves foolishly because his motive in dealing with us is love alone. This is the Good News of God's Kingdom to which Jesus wants us to be converted and in which we are called to believe.

The theological message in all these parables is the same. They show the incomprehensible goodness and kindness of God towards all human beings when the Kingdom will come in its glory. A new order is starting now based not on justice but on God's goodness and kindness. Justice becomes subordinated to this kindness and compassion of God. In the Parable of the Laborers in the Vineyard Jesus is demonstrating that all human beings stand in need of God's kindness and compassion and these will undoubtedly be given to each one at the end, when the Kingdom comes in its fullness.

Commenting on the Parable of the Laborers in the Vineyard Joachim Jeremias concludes:

> God is depicted as acting like an employer who has compassion for the unemployed and their families. He gives to publicans and sinners a share, all undeserved, in his Kingdom. So will he deal with them on the Last Day. That, says Jesus, is what he is like; and because he is like that, so am I; since I am acting under his order and in his stead. Will you then murmur against God's goodness? That is the core of Jesus' vindication of the Gospel: Look what God is like - all goodness. (*Parables of the Kingdom*)

This was Jesus' vision that determined his whole life. For this vision he lived, suffered and ultimately died. It has been called the 'agapeic vision' of the New Testament. With this vision Jesus offended the just of his time. Jesus' proclamation of God as unconditional love was always upsetting. It upset all standards in so far as he saw salvation coming, not from what human beings would do, but from the acceptance of a "God who comes to love us first."

The real content of Jesus' message of the Kingdom consists therefore, in his image of God: God loves every human being with UNCONDITIONAL LOVE. Conversion to the Kingdom message of Jesus means therefore, first of all, a conversion to the image of God that Jesus revealed to us. What is the true nature of God?

> God is love...This is how God showed his love for us: he sent his only Son into the world that we might have life through him. This is what love is: it is not that we have loved God, but that he loved us first and sent his Son to be our Savior (1 Jn 4:9).

The God whom Jesus revealed as unconditional love was ultimately so offensive to the just of the time that they put him away for being a 'blasphemer' (Mt 26:59-66). This image of God that Jesus came to reveal in its fullness, already runs like a thread through the entire Old Testament. After having examined the whole Old Testament under this aspect, one Old Testament exegete sums up his findings as follows:

> The most important of all the distinctive ideas of the Old Testament is God's steady and extraordinary persistence in continuing to love wayward Israel in spite of Israel's waywardness. It is His persistent love that will not let Israel go, a love that not all of man's weakness and sinfulness and stubbornness can destroy. His love never wavers, never ceases. This is an Old Testament truth of permanent force and validity, one that we cannot dispense with (L.Morris, *Testament of Love*).

A few Scripture texts may illustrate this point even further:

> I have loved you with an everlasting love; therefore I have continued my faithfulness to you (Jr 31:1).

God will never give you up: the constancy of his love depends on what he is and not on what you are or on how you behave.

> For I know well the plans I have in mind for you, says the Lord, plans for your welfare not for your woe. Plans to give you a future full of hope. When you look for me, you will find me. Yes, when you seek me with all your heart, you will find me with you," says the Lord, "and I will change your lot" (Jr 29:11-14).

But the people of Jerusalem said, 'The Lord has abandoned us. He has forgotten us.' Can a woman forget her baby and not love the child she bore? Even if a mother should forget her child, I will never forget you. I have written your name on the palms of my hands (Is 49:14-16).

Here we have the most touching expression of divine love in the entire Bible. The figure is not the usual figure of paternal love, but the rarer figure of maternal love. The same attitude of God towards us is also found in Hosea 11:1-9 where God's love proves stronger than his vengeance. The love of God underlies the whole of the Old Testament. If we do not recognize that as its foundation, nothing in the Old Testament makes much sense.

Probably the most glorious scene in the entire Old Testament is the portrayal of Moses on Mount Sinai, holding the two tablets of the Law and hearing the thunderous sound of the Lord passing by. It is here that Yahweh reveals his true name and being:

Having come down in a cloud, the Lord stood with Moses there and proclaimed his name, "Lord." Thus the Lord passed before Moses and cried out, "The Lord, the Lord, a merciful and gracious God, slow to anger and rich in kindness and fidelity, continuing his kindness for a thousand generations and forgiving wickedness and crime and sin..." Moses at once bowed down to the ground and worshipped (Ex 34:3-4).

What is important here is the setting in which Yahweh reveals his very being. Moses is holding the Ten Commandments and God reveals to him who the God is to whom the Israelites submit themselves in the Covenant: **a God of mercy and full of compassion**. The Torah is to be lived and interpreted in the light of such a God.

Jesus came to reveal the fullness of God's limitless love for everyone. The following story is told of a Moslem theologian from Tunis who was asked to translate the Parable of the Prodigal Son into Arabic. When he brought forth the translation, so the story goes, he wept as he read it, for he had not imagined that God would have such tender love for his creatures. A Jewish scholar who commented on the three parables of Luke 15 had this to say:

The virtues of repentance are gloriously praised in the Rabbinical literature, but this direct search for and appeal to the sinner are NEW and moving notes of high importance and significance. — Jesus is not passing on a commonplace idea of the teaching of his day. He is saying something of which his contemporaries knew nothing as he proclaims the truth that God is a seeking God, one who reaches out in love to the sinner and brings him home. (C.G. Montefiore in Morris, *Testament of Love*)

What is My Image of God?

How do I relate to God? Do I believe that Luke's three parables — the Prodigal Son, the Lost Sheep and the Lost Coin — in which Luke expresses God's relationship with us in Christ, convey the true nature of God's love for us? Do I really believe this or not? Do I believe that God searches for every human being in the same way as a shepherd does for the lost sheep? Do I believe that God is like a father who sees his lost son from afar and goes to meet him, and that this alone gives the son the strength to go ahead and meet his father?

Luke 15 sets a decision before me. Do I really believe that God is, day after day, on the way to meet me? For many people God is what a parachute is for a pilot: something he must have, but hopes he will never have to use.

Our greatest sin against such incomprehensible love is most probably our indifference. It leaves us cold. Theoretically we might be convinced of God's unconditional love, yet, it is only in our actual living, the way we relate to ourselves, to others and the world, that we manifest what kind of God we have accepted for ourselves as well as what king of God we really worship. This brings us back to the question which Jesus constantly asks anyone who wants to follow him: Where, in the last analysis, does your heart lie? Who or what rules your life? "For where your treasure is, there will your heart be also" (Mt 6:21; Lk 12:34).

A New Image

To move towards life-giving attitudes there are some real questions you will have to ask yourself: Can I imagine for myself a new future with new possibilities and new potentials? Can I imagine for myself a more fulfilled ministry? Can I become reconciled with my past in such a way that I will not remain enclosed in it for the rest of my life but can imagine myself, others, the world around me and God differently than I have up to now? Can I transcend my present life, the result of my past, and give it a new direction?

All this depends on whether I am able to create new images, whether I can envision new possibilities for my future. There lies the core and essence of all conversion: to gather the past into the present and to open myself to a new future which can be different from what the past would predict. A person who has no visions anymore, who cannot dream of a future different from the past and present, will never know what conversion is.

Where do new visions come from? Who can stir my dried up imagination? Who can give me a new image of what I realistically could be? Who can present to me the ideal self in a way that it becomes once again a new challenge to my real self? Scripture tells us that it is the Holy Spirit who gives "visions to the young and dreams to the old" (Ac 2:17). Conversion is, therefore, not something that I can do but a gift of the Holy Spirit. All I can do is to ask for a vision of myself that is realizable, what God could do for me if I would let him do it.

The question that constantly confronts us in the face of this vision of Jesus is the same that people asked St. Peter on Pentecost, "What shall we do?" (Ac 2:37) The answer Peter gave is the same that Jesus gave his audience when he first proclaimed the Kingdom:

1. Convert (Mk 1:15)

This means not first of all a turning away from something but a turning towards something. Jesus asks you to let yourself be turned around; to let the power of the Kingdom into your life; to open yourself to its influence. Ultimately it means to let the never-heard-of Good News of God's unbelievable love for you enter your life.

2. Become a child (Mk 10:15; Lk 18:17)

This is another way of understanding conversion. Being "like a child" means one has nothing to give, nothing to show in order to gain the Kingdom. The child opens up a vast area of Kingdom qualities: trust, humility, obedience, and a forgiving spirit. Instead of seeking power and status, the Kingdom requires that we humble ourselves, shed our self-imposed importance and worldly values, and find our true vocation in obedient service to God. Jesus' demand of 'becoming a child' expresses the necessity for adults to make a new beginning, to have a new responsiveness and openness to God and others. 'Being a child' indicates more than change of direction. It implies new life and rebirth and comes close to the more explicit Johannine imagery:

> Jesus answered and said to him, "Amen, amen, I say to you, no one can see the Kingdom of God without being born from above." Nicodemus said to him, "How can a person once grown old be born again? Surely he cannot

reenter his mother's womb and be born again, can he?" Jesus answered, "Amen, amen, I say to you, no one can enter the Kingdom of God without being born of water and Spirit" (Jn 3:3-5).

3. Let the Spirit well up from within you

In the Gospel of John Jesus employs the image of a well that is within to symbolize the Holy Spirit (Jn 4:14ff). Conversion here means to let the life-giving waters of the Holy Spirit well up from within us and bring us to life. In Luke 17:20 Jesus speaks about the Kingdom not as coming in signs and wonders but as the Kingdom "within us." The Early Church Fathers understood this to mean: the Kingdom is within our reach, it is so close and intimate that we can take hold of it if we really want it.

There were once two monks who were browsing together through a musty tome. There they read that at the very outermost limits of this world, one could find a place where heaven and earth met and the Kingdom of God began. They decided to search for this land and not to return until they had found it. They wandered through the world, facing innumerable dangers and suffering untold deprivations; everything in fact that one would associate with such a venture. They overcame every temptation to turn back from their goal. They knew there would be a door at the end of their journey. One had only to knock, and he would find himself in the Kingdom of God. And so it was — at the end, they found what they were looking for. They knocked on the door, and with quaking hearts saw it open before them. And when they entered, they found themselves at home, standing in the cell of their monastery. They looked at one another in amazement. And in that moment, the realization dawned on them: The place where the Kingdom of God begins is indeed to be found on earth, but in the position and circumstances of life that God's providence assigns to us. (P. Jacobi, *Damit unsere Leben gelingen kann*)

Whoever drinks the water (the Holy Spirit) that I will give him will never be thirsty again. For the water that I will give him will become in him a spring which will provide living water, and give him eternal life (Jn 4:14).

4. Let Christ make his home in your heart

Paul on his part sees conversion happening when Christ is taking shape in us (Ep 3:14-19). For him indwelling is the endpoint towards which all conversion must be directed. Conversion means a turning to Christ, accepting salvation from him. According to Colossians 1 all human beings are created in the image of Christ. They carry in themselves his image as their true "hidden self". As Paul tells us, "The mystery is: Christ lives in you the glory to come" (Col 1:27). One could compare this with a "watermark" that we find on stamps or bank notes. Conversion from this perspective means to let Christ take shape in us and to lead the person from mere image into likeness.

5. Thinking differently

According to the Greek word *metanoia* conversion means to "think differently", to look at reality the way Jesus did; it means to accept his perspective and his "frame of reference" to use his "eyeglasses" when looking at the world and human reality.

Keep in mind that the Gospel is always brand new, always Good News for you and me, always a never heard of, unbelievable reality that can give your life an unimagined future and a lasting security. It is something to get excited about at any time. Conversion for us means to set out anew and look for the hidden treasure, and once we have found it, to go and sell everything we have to buy the field in which the treasure is buried (Mt 13:44).

Is this not asking a little too much, you might ask? Why should this retreat make a difference in comparison with all the others I have made so far?

This reminds me of an experience I had some years ago. I was asked by a bishop to give a retreat to his priests. He had persuaded them to leave their parishes for a week by advertising the name of the retreat-master. When I arrived, one of the priests who was obviously not very impressed with the bishop's press campaign, came up to me and said, "So you are the hired man who is finally going to convert us! Well, let me tell you, I have made more than twenty retreats in my life. Do you think this one can be so different that I will actually be changed? You must have a lot of self confidence and faith, Father!"

As a result of this incident I have since put a little more stress on asking the Holy Spirit for his guidance and help in preparing to preach a retreat than on my own efforts. Who am I to change a person's heart?

Like that priest, many of us might have experienced many attempts to change our lives and we seem to have ended up right back where we started. Too many flowers have withered leaving us without any fruit. Who will blame us if there is a deep rooted doubt in each of us as to whether or not we can become what we really want to be?

Some exegetes tell us that John in his Gospel depicts in Nicodemus the typical 'churchman' or religious person. After leading a spiritual and religious life for many years, Nicodemus knew what was possible, what progress one could still make and where one would have to be contented with what one has achieved. Nicodemus had found a "liveable balance" between the values of the Torah and the daily need for accommodation. He had mastered the bearable tension between the "real self and the ideal self." Yet, he sensed in Jesus' message a way that could lead him on to heights he dared only dream about. But Jesus' message sounded too radical. Therefore he asks, "How can I grow further? I am an old man with ingrained habits, with a definite view of reality, with a settled self image. I cannot overturn everything I have built up so painstakingly and with which I feel quite comfortable. What do you want me to do?" Jesus' only reply is, "Nicodemus, if you would only know the power of the Kingdom and let its Spirit into your life, unimaginable things could happen to you" (Jn 3:1-17).

Are Nicodemus' objections not accurate? Do we not all often feel that the demands of the Gospel are just too idealistic? Who can live them? Yet, it is my experience with priests and religious that no matter how far they have drifted away, how badly they have deteriorated or become stagnated, deep down in their hearts they all long for a real unique and total commitment to the Lord.

So the question each of us struggles with is: can I really change? Can I still be converted to the Lord in the way I desire deep within me, in spite of all the negative experiences in my life that have led me to settle for somewhere in between, after I have pulled down my ideal self to a level where it poses no challenge anymore?

I could on this point be encouraged by the charismatics, whose main aim is to change their lives and they work at it with great tenacity. They have that "expectant faith" which holds that conversion can happen by praying with others.

Some Attitudes Toward Change:

There are a number of attitudes which hinder the possibility of change and which we should, therefore, think about:

A FATALISTIC ATTITUDE: "It is useless anyway. I have tried too often to believe that change is still possible." At the root of this attitude is a subtle despair and, strangely enough, it is quite common among many. Some say,

"Well, there was always some progress after each retreat, I will settle for the same old thing this time."

A COMPLACENT ATTITUDE: One can take the attitude of complacency by saying, "I don't need a conversion. I am satisfied with what I am." In that case you could be compared with an over-ripe apple; the only future is to rot! Or one could say, "I am O.K., You are O.K.," as the title of Thomas Harris' book goes. A Christian version of the book title would read, "I am not O.K., You are not O.K., but that's O.K." To be jolted out of this attitude some traumatic events are often needed. The story of the man born blind in John 9:1-7 is a beautiful illustration of such an attitude. God has to put clay on our eyes and blur our vision before he can heal us. (An interpretation given by St. Augustine)

A PRAGMATIC ATTITUDE: "Since I am already in this retreat I might as well give it another try."

On a Good Friday while hearing confession, a man entered the confessional and told me, "Father, to be honest, I don't want to go to confession." I asked him, "But why are you coming then?" His response was, "Do you see that woman outside there, it's my wife; if I want peace during these Easter days, I better climb into this box." "Well," I replied, "Since you are already here, why don't you make it a real confession?" After some hesitation he said, "I might as well do so." Years later he told me, "Father John, it was that confession on that memorable Good Friday, forced on me by my wife, that truly changed my entire life."

Real conversion is possible for me only if I can imagine such a God, if I can envision such a love for me now as real and actual. Am I willing to let this image of God into my life? If I do, my relationship with and my experience of myself, of my friends and relatives, of institutions like the Church and my religious congregation, of nature and the environment will definitely change too. Can I imagine for myself a different form of life than that which I am living now? Or am I like Nicodemus who could not believe anymore that one can still begin anew (Jn 3:16)? Nicodemus is described in the Gospel as a man with little confidence in the recreative power of God's Spirit. Jesus tells him: if you would only trust in God's immense love that comes with me into the world, unimaginable things could happen to you. God's care and love for you is also expressed in these texts:

> I made you... in my own image and likeness and when I made you I saw that you are good (Gn 1:27;31).

You are my work of art (Ep 2:10).

You...are part of my household (Ep 2:22).

You.. reflect like a mirror the brightness of the Lord and grow brighter as you turn into the image that you reflect, this is my work (2 Co 3:10).

Do I really live out of this unconditional love of God for me or do I not? Some experiences in my own life have led me not only to know that love more profoundly but to realize some of its implications in my daily life.

When I was teaching in a seminary in the Philippines a novice who was an active member of a charismatic group, came to me one day and claimed that he had a prophetic message for me, "You want to be generous with the Lord," he said, "there is no doubt that you are, but what is really wrong with you is that you do not dare to let the Lord take over your life. You want to stay in control and you are afraid to let the Spirit take over. Because in the moment he does, you would not know what might happen. Of that you are afraid...."

He was right. The step into such a freedom seems so difficult for us. It is as if we would lose the ground on which we stand. But is this not why Jesus came: to give us an AMEN to stand on — God's unconditional love?

I once met a Sister who had been working for 40 years in a leper colony. She was known to be a very joyful and lively person, and so I asked her, "How is it that you are such a joyful and inspiring person in spite of all the continuously hard and often frustrating work you have to do?" She answered, "Well, Father, it took twenty five years of religious life before I suddenly realized that God truly loves me. That experience changed my whole way of life. From that day on I became a different person. And only if you had known me before could you appreciate what a different person I have become.."

Conversion, then, would really mean that I let the theoretical knowledge that God loves me travel from my head to my heart and that I start living in response to this love which I experience more and more as the ultimate source of my being. His love for me has to become increasingly the only motive for all my prayer, work and action. Then my life will begin to become a response to that incomprehensible love for me.

Questions for Reflection:

1. What image of God guides my life and inspires my action?

2. How do I look at myself, my friends and relatives, at institutions, at nature and climate? Is it from the perspective of one who knows that God loves me unconditionally?

3 Can I imagine for myself a future different from the present, a future with new possibilities and new potentials based on my having a different image of God?

4. Am I convinced that I can transcend my present life, the result of my past and give it a new direction because I have experienced God's incomprehensible, unconditional love for me?

Story for Reflection:

OSU, THE KING: AN IMPOSSIBLE RELIGION

He was a great dancer. Osu the King, they called him, although poor and without any influence in the tribe. However, his ancestors had been great kings, and he took pride in honoring them and showing in his demeanor he was well aware of his royal heritage. I saw him dancing during an ordination ceremony of a young man from his village. He had a way of dancing that spoke of total commitment to what he was doing. They told me he clung to his ancestral faith, even when the whole tribe had converted to Christianity. But then one day Osu went to the priest with the request: "I would like to become a Christian; please, instruct me in the faith." For two years he sat with the other catechumens to prepare for baptism. When the day, on which he had to ask to be accepted into the Christian community drew near, he again went to the priest. "I cannot let myself be baptized and become a Christian," he said. "I am not capable of being one." The priest, in turn, looked at Osu with amazement. "But Osu, why can you not? You are as worthy as anyone of your group to ask for baptism." Then came the reply, "Over the two years of instruction in the Christian faith, I have made a serious attempt to believe and to live what I have been taught. Now I realize that the Christian religion is not for people on this earth, it is too good to believe. If I should find out one day that it can be lived I will come back." Then he just turned around and walked out.

The problem we often have with God's unconditional love for us is not that we find it too hard to believe but rather that it is too good to accept as true for us personally.

Poem for Reflection

The **Kingdom of God** in its fullness is **like a DREAM** that God is dreaming within each of us. This is God's dream which is the heart of our vocation:

> And the Lord God said:
> I myself will dream a dream within you.
> Good dreams come from me you know.
> My dreams seem impossible,
> not too practical.
> Not for the cautious man and woman.
> A little risky sometimes,
> a trifle brash perhaps.
> Some of my friends prefer
> to rest more comfortably,
> in sounder sleep,
> with visionless eyes.
> But from those who share my dreams,
> I ask a little patience
> a little humor,
> some small courage,
> and a listening heart.
> I will do the rest.
> Then they will risk,
> and wonder at their daring;
> run and marvel at their speed;
> Build, and stand in awe at the beauty
> of their building.
>
> You will meet me often as you work:
> in your companions, who share your risk:
> in friends, who believe in you enough
> to lend their own dreams,
> their own hands,
> their own hearts,
> to your building;
> In the people who will find your doorway,
> stay awhile, and walk away
> knowing they too can find a dream...

There will be sun-filled days,
and sometimes it will rain.
A little variety!
both come from me.

So come now, be content.

It is my dream you dream:
  my house you build;
  my caring you witness;
  my love you share;

And this is the heart of the matter.

(Composed by Sr. Charity in C. Futrell, *The Challenge of Ministry*)

CONVERSION: CHANGE OF SECURITY

Introduction

Real conversion occurs when I let myself be turned towards the Kingdom and let its power in. Or, to use our other image, "I let its power well up in me". Or, "I put on those new eyeglasses that enable me to get things into focus."

Don't you understand! God is running after you day and night as though he has nothing else to do but simply to occupy himself with you (Catherine of Siena).

What is this power of the Kingdom? It is God's unconditional love for me. Jesus came to tell us who God really is, and he urged us, tried to persuade us to surrender ourselves into the hand of such a God. Jesus pleaded God's cause, he pleaded for God's love. His message was, "Open yourself to this totally new, unheard of, unbelievably amazing reality, surrender fully to this God who is Father."

Jesus' whole mission was to convert us to this God. He came to heal our imagination of any wrong image of God. The Parable of the Lost Sheep demonstrates this most beautifully. God acts "irrationally" when it comes to someone who is lost. It is not reason, but love that moves him. For instance, no real shepherd would leave ninety-nine sheep in the desert, i.e., expose them to wolves and lions and run after one lost sheep. This same attitude we find in the story of the Prodigal Son when the Father explains to his older son, "Can you not understand, your younger brother was lost and now he is found. We just had to celebrate with all we have!" (Lk 15:32).

As stated before, the opposite of love is not hatred nor fear but indifference. We just don't think God could really be like that. Real conversion is possible and will take place if I can imagine such a God, if I can envision such a love for me now as real and actual. It is not difficult for most of us to accept such an image of God theoretically. We have heard about it in thousands of sermons and conferences, but the real test comes when I am asked to entrust my whole existence completely and unconditionally to such a God. It is only the reflection on our actual living, the way we look at and relate to ourselves, to others and to the world that will reveal to us what image of God image we have accepted for ourselves and what kind of God we worship. Conversion means, therefore, a change of lords; as Jesus put it, "You cannot serve two masters" (Mt 6:24).

Who is the master of my heart? Where in the last analysis does my heart lie? "For where your treasure is, there will your heart be also" (Mt 6:22; Lk 12:34). What Jesus is asking in these texts is: "What is it that gives meaning to your life? What is your ultimate security?"

The Need for Acceptance and Love

All human beings cry out for love, acceptance and recognition as foundations to stand on. We all know from experience that recognition and acceptance by others are prior to achievement and usefulness. We need the former for our own security. If we do not receive recognition and acceptance, we adopt all kinds of other measures to make ourselves feel secure. We direct these security measures towards our fellow human beings and even towards God because we do not find the acceptance and recognition we need in order to be ourselves. The security measures we often take arise from the most important basic instincts: i.e., the ones that emerge from the human need for prestige, power and pleasure (H. Muehlen, *Charismatic Theology*).

These needs are the expression of what is called the most disastrous effect of original sin which is our ingrained tendency to have, to accumulate, to possess and to dominate in order to make ourselves secure.

1. PRESTIGE — WITHDRAWAL

If I am not accepted by others, I will try anything to gain that acceptance and recognition. Then people will have to accept me and I won't be hurt. I do not seek their acceptance of me as a human person. I find my security not in that recognition but in my profession, my skill, my work; in short, in my own achievement, which people cannot overlook. The danger is that I do not trust persons who can give me true security, but that I will look for security in myself. The opposite of wanting recognition is WITHDRAWAL. Its effect is the same. I might withdraw into myself to protect myself against disappointment and hurt.

If I don't take others, myself and even God too seriously, I cannot get hurt. Withdrawal is basically a security measure taken to avoid the loss of meaning of my life. I do not trust anyone.

2. POWER — SUBMISSIVENESS

To strive after power, possession and superiority can easily become another security measure. Jesus saw this danger. His warnings against riches and possessions are stern (Mk 10: 23-25). By having more, I think that I am more. If I am powerful, no one can touch me and I cannot get easily hurt. I have secured myself by what I possess. I do not have to depend on anyone. The acceptance and recognition I need I can buy or will get through my status. Once again, it is my own doing that gives me security.

In the seminary we had a Brother who had the key to the community store. No one could get even a piece of soap without first recognizing the importance of this Brother. Only then would his key open the door. By chance I was present on the day when the Brother was to retire and hand over responsibility for his beloved store. While I was sitting with him reminiscing over the past, the superior of the house entered and said, "Well, Brother, now you can spend the rest of your days in peace, with no one to bother you. You really deserve to be released from this job after so many years of faithful service. And now, would you give me the keys to all these cabinets here?" The Brother became white as a sheet and with trembling hands handed the keys over to the superior. When the superior was gone, the Brother started to cry and stammered, "Father John, now I am nothing anymore. They have taken the last thing from me that gave me any importance in this community."

The question you might ask yourself is the following: What is the 'key' I control and what recognition do I demand before people can get what this key can provide?

SUBMISSIVENESS, the opposite of power, possession and superiority, can also be a pure security measure. If I do whatever I am asked to do, I am secure; they cannot hurt me. One can even believe that this attitude is the best security before God. Some Jewish leaders at the time of Jesus believed that God would be compelled to give them the Kingdom. They tried to secure themselves against God by keeping the Law.

The following incident helped me recognize some of these attitudes in action.

I had an aunt who became a Seventh-Day-Adventist. It really upset my father when he saw her preaching on the street opposite our village Church. He would never call her by name but referred to her as "that woman who is a disgrace to the whole family." I told my father that he should not be so hard on her. After all, she was devoted and convinced in her faith, as evidenced by how hard she was willing to work to convert others. One day, after another outburst of anger from my father directed at this "disgrace to the family," I asked him whether he was so sure that my renegade aunt might not end up even higher in heaven than we.

Then my father gave me, his priest son, a lecture in theology as he understood it. He said, "All my life I have tried to be a good Catholic, and at times it was very hard. I have never missed Sunday Mass. I have gone to confession every first Friday. I have supported the Catholic faith in all kinds of movements. I have raised five children and tried my best to make them good Catholics. Your being a priest, I hope, proves me right. Now, you are trying to tell me that this renegade woman who left the Church and ran after such religious nonsense, might one day be "higher in heaven" than I? What kind of theology did they teach you?"

I did not say a word. But later, it made me wonder what Jesus might have said to my father and my aunt when they met in heaven after death. I imagine the encounter might have been something like this: Jesus looked at my father, and paraphrasing the words addressed to the elder brother in the Parable of the Prodigal Son, said with gentle irony: "Why are you so upset that I love her as much as I love you? After all, she is your sister."

3. PLEASURE — SELF CONTEMPT

Pleasure can become a security measure. If I enjoy myself, nothing can upset me. The usual compensations for loss of prestige, acceptance and recognition are drink, drugs, stimulants, over-eating, gambling or sex. The misuse of one's sexuality is normally a search for security, a turning in on oneself to safeguard oneself. All these are attempts to secure meaning for myself without which I cannot live.

The opposite of pleasure is contempt for the world and for oneself. He who does not succeed in enjoying life, easily disassociates himself from himself in unjustified self-criticism and reproaches. His or her motto is: What I cannot enjoy, I despise.

The sad fact is that we all live in a sin-permeated world and that means that even the most perfect parents can never give their children that full acceptance, recognition and love they cry out for. The result is that we all carry within us to some degree a mistrust of others and with it, of the God we came to know through our parents.

The range of security measures that we can invent is almost infinite and often amazingly subtle. It is here that we might feel most the effects of original sin, which consist in having lost the ultimate security on which we stand as creatures. We cannot live without securing for ourselves meaning in our lives. The question is: Where can I find my security? Do I seek it by protecting myself from any possible hurt, disappointment, or loss of meaning; by making myself independent of others who can give me that recognition I need, but who can also hurt me? If I do so, it is because deep down in my heart, I don't trust them. But since I cannot live without trust, I have to find meaning in my own security measures. After all, since I have nowhere to stand within myself, I have to hold on to something!

Henry Nouwen, in his book WITH OPEN HANDS, has a beautiful story about a mentally disturbed woman which clearly illustrates this point. The woman was brought to a psychiatric center. Nouwen writes:

She was wild, swinging at everything in sight, and scaring everyone so much that the doctors had to take everything away from her. But there was one small coin which she gripped in her fist and would not give up. In fact it took two men to pry open her hand. It was as though she would lose her very self along with the coin. If they deprived her of that last possession, she would have nothing more, and be nothing more. This is what she feared.

The question to ask yourself is: What do you have gripped tightly in your fist? What is it that you would not dare give up from fear of losing yourself?

Knowing Oneself to be Secure

This brings us back to our theme. Conversion means making "a change in the sources of my securities". The Hebrew word for 'faith' is AMEN, which literally means TO KNOW ONESELF TO BE SECURE. Isaiah, the prophet of faith, shows in particular that faith and existence belong together. For him to live by faith is the only possible mode of existence; it radically excludes any autonomy for a human being or any commitment to any other god.

If you do not stand by me, you will not stand at all (Is 7:9). Or: If your faith is not enduring you will not endure.

Scholars regard this phrase as the most developed and mature definition of faith in the whole Old Testament. Our only security is God alone. He is our AMEN (Is 65:16), who fulfills our deepest need for acceptance, recognition and security. In Rev 3:14, Jesus is called "our Amen", meaning he is the one in whom we are secure, accepted, recognized and loved.

What can we ever say to such wonderful things as these? If God is on our side, who can ever be against us? Since he did not spare even his own Son but gave him up for us all, won't he also surely give us everything else? Who then can ever keep Christ's love from us? When we have trouble or calamity, when we are hunted down or destroyed, is it because he doesn't love us anymore? And if we are hungry, or penniless, or in danger, or threatened with death, has God deserted us? For I am convinced that nothing can ever separate us from his love. Death can't and life can't. The angels won't, and all the powers of hell itself cannot keep God's love away. Our fear for today, our worries about tomorrow, or where we are - high above the sky, or in the deepest ocean - nothing will ever be able to separate us from the love of God demonstrated by our Lord Jesus Christ when he died for us (Rm 8:31-32; 35; 38-39).

Conversion in negative terms would mean to give up all gods, to stop searching for security, recognition and acceptance in my own self and to open myself fully to Christ alone as my new Lord. Sin is a person's constant search to find security in false sources. Sin is mistrust of God's love; it is the refusal to let God's Kingdom into my life.

Paul Tillich defines faith as "Courage to accept acceptance." That means: I accept the fact that God has accepted me, that he recognizes me, and that he loves me, not on the basis of what I have, but out of pure love. In this love I find security, meaning and joy.

How can I discover this love in my life?

There is a simple exercise I would like you to do. Put yourself into the presence of God and then go through your life as you have lived it thus far and reflect on all the good things you have experienced and people you met in your life and try to discover behind these events and persons God's love for you. After all, he is the true source of all goodness. In doing this you will get a feel for the all-pervasive presence of his love in your whole life. Only that can lead you to a deeper trust in this love and change the way you look at yourself and at the whole of reality. At times you might not feel anything and will have to rely only on your faith conviction. But if you repeat this exercise regularly you will discover who it is who directs your life.

In order to go on receiving, deepening and living this unconditional love of God in my life, I ask myself once in a while, "What would I have liked to have achieved in my life when I come to face death?" The more the thought of God's love for me fascinates me, the more I will understand that a successful life means living in the realization of this unconditional love of God for me. The more I do this the more I will feel called to surrender myself more and more to this love. I would hope that my death might be an act of unconditional surrender to this love. This is what it means to live a successful life.

This wish came to me during my novitiate years and was the result of the following experience. As a novice, I once met an old China missionary, a holy man who had been thrown out of China by the communists. One day while I was talking with him, a lady whom he knew well came to visit. They started chatting about different things, and eventually the topic shifted to the reality of growing old and the prospect of soon standing before God. The lady reminded the old missionary that he had nothing to fear. He should think of all the merits he had collected in those forty years of hard missionary work in China. What a great welcome he would receive as a reward for so many good works! The old missionary looked very kindly at his lady friend and said something I have never forgotten. "Mary, when I die and get up there to face judgment, if the good Lord does not mention China, let me tell you, I will keep my mouth shut too. I shall put all my trust in his love for me, a love he has shown to me time and again throughout my life."

The great message that we have to carry, as ministers of God's word and followers of Jesus, is that God loves us not because of what we do or accomplish, but because God has created and redeemed us in love and has chosen us to proclaim that love as the true source of all human life. (H. Nouwen, *In the Name of Jesus*)

Questions for Reflection:

At the beginning we asked: Can I imagine for myself a new future with new possibilities perhaps a more fulfilled, perhaps a more meaningful, a more joyful life? The answer depends on the following points:

1. Am I willing to let the Holy Spirit produce in me new visions and images of God as Christ has presented Him to us?

2. Am I willing to entrust myself to this God of Jesus Christ and find in him my security, recognition and acceptance?

There are some signs that can indicate whether or not I have undergone a conversion - I will experience in myself:

— a new sense and taste for prayer.
— a new awareness of God's presence in my life.
— a new taste for Holy Scripture as a word of God
  addressed to me personally.
— a new view of my apostolate.

Story for Reflection:

THE STREAM

A stream, from its source in the far-off mountains, passing through every kind and description of countryside, at last reached the sands of the desert. Just as it had crossed every other barrier, the stream tried to cross this one, but found that as fast as it ran into the sand, its waters disappeared. It was convinced, however, that its destiny was to cross the desert, and yet there was no way. Now a hidden voice, coming from the desert itself, whispered, "The wind crosses the desert and so can the stream."

The stream objected that it was dashing itself against the sand only to be absorbed, that the wind could fly, and this was why it could cross the desert. Said the desert, "By hurling in your own accustomed way you cannot get across. You will either disappear or become a marsh. You must allow the wind to carry you over to your destination."

But how can this happen? "By allowing yourself to be absorbed by the wind." This idea was not acceptable to the stream. After all, it had never been absorbed before. It did not want to lose its individuality. And, once having lost it, how was one to know that it could ever be regained?

"The wind," said the sand, "performs this function. It takes up the water, carries it over the desert, and then lets it fall again. Falling as rain, the water again becomes a river."

"How can I know this is true?"

"It is so, and if you do not believe it, you cannot become more than a quagmire, and even that could take many, many years; and it certainly is not the same as a stream."

"But can I not remain the same stream that I am today?"

"You cannot in either case remain so, "the whisper said. "Your essential part is carried away and forms a stream again. You are called what you are even today because you do not know which part of you is the essential one."

When he heard this, certain echoes began to rise in the thoughts of the stream. Dimly, he remembered a state in which he or some part of him had been held in the arms of the wind. He also remembered — or did he? — that this was the real thing, not necessarily the obvious thing to do.

And the stream raised his vapor into the welcoming arms of the wind which gently and easily bore it upward and along, letting it fall softly as soon as they reached the roof of a mountain many, many miles away. And because he had had his doubts, the stream was able to remember and record more strongly in his mind the details of that experience. He reflected, "Yes, now I have learned my true identity."

(Paul J. Wharton)

BELIEVE: TRUST IN THE KINGDOM NOW

Introduction

We talked about the central message of Jesus, a message which includes all his actions, all his symbolic gestures and all his teaching and preaching. This message is ultimately about God's unconditional love for his creatures. Since the coming of Jesus this love is offered to each human being at any moment and in any place wherever he or she may live and regardless of the faith he or she may pledge allegiance to.

This love makes itself present and available as a 'dynamic power' with only one basic aim and goal: to transform the whole of creation into the New Heaven and the New Earth in which every human being that has ever lived will find ultimate salvation. The whole process of human history and the whole evolutionary process of nature is moving towards this final fulfillment of God's grand design for creation.

This is the "indicative mood" of Jesus' message: THE KINGDOM IS HERE. Jesus connected two imperatives with this proclamation, two demands that remain inseparable from the message itself: REPENT AND BELIEVE.

In the last two conferences, we talked about the first demand of the Kingdom: REPENT. In this conference we will talk about the second demand: BELIEVE.

The basic meaning of "believe" is expressed in the Hebrew language by the word AMEN, which means, literally, TO KNOW TO BE SECURE. As we saw earlier, the Kingdom is the ultimate security which God offers us in his Son. With His demand for our faith in the Kingdom Jesus offers us a rock to stand on, a security to rely on, and a love we can trust in without any fear or anxiety (Rm 8:32f).

I would like to present four aspects of faith which are worth meditating on, particularly in our time. To believe means: (1) to accept a particular worldview; (2) not to see, but to trust, and therefore to walk at times in darkness; (3) to be constantly on guard not to lose the treasure of the Kingdom; and, (4) to be constantly directed towards the future coming of the Lord, who will bring salvation to its completion.

1. TO BELIEVE MEANS TO ACCEPT A PARTICULAR WORLD-VIEW

A believer does not regard all that he or she sees, hears and experiences, all that can be touched and examined, as the whole of reality. A believer has access to reality as a whole which supersedes any ordinary way of seeing and understanding things.

Faith provides me with a special dimension with which I can approach reality without doing any violence to it. Faith provides me with a depth-dimension which lets me see and understand reality from a deep level and perspective. Faith gives me a tool, so to speak, which enables me to see and to judge the world which surrounds me in the way it wants to be seen and understood. It gives me a particular worldview.

Faith provides me with the certainty that, in spite of all negative experiences, our world is not given to absurdity, not left to blind destiny, but that behind all dark and sometimes incomprehensible complexity, a meaning is hidden which keeps the whole of creation in balance. This brutal, bleeding, sometimes hopeless and sin-permeated world is carried in the caring hands of God who loves unconditionally. It was this faith that preserved saints from falling into despair or committing suicide. Terese of Lisieux writes in her "LAST WORDS", "If I had not had faith, I would have committed suicide."

A commercial about Polaroid eyeglasses filmed for television some years ago gave me a down to earth example of the dimension which faith brings to our human way of looking at things. The commercial showed a swimming pool in which two beautiful girls were swimming and diving. Because of the glare of the sun reflected on the surface, one could not really see the bathing beauties. So the viewer was offered a pair of Polaroid eyeglasses. With their help, he could then clearly see through the water without being bothered by the glare.

As trivial as the example might be, it does illustrate the point. Our faith enables us to bypass the surface glare, to grasp the depth of reality, and to see things as they really are. It helps us to discover the real nature and importance of events in the setting of God's final plan for this world and the direction he is giving to human history.

Another example:

Some years ago NASA sent into space a satellite, programmed to get as close at Mars as possible before sending pictures back to earth. The satellite reached its destination. The command was given to start taking pictures. But then they discovered a magnetic dust storm raging on Mars that made it impossible to photograph the surface of the planet. It was at this point that scientists arranged a combination of lenses and filters for the camera which made it possible to penetrate the obstacles and obtain excellent pictures of the planet and its surface.

To have faith means to be equipped with the right lenses and filters. With them in place, we are able to get beneath the surface of things, to see through any dust or obstacles that hinder a clear view, and to understand and judge reality accordingly.

Faith means ultimately to accept the worldview which Jesus had. It means to look at the world through his eyes. He alone had the right view. He demonstrated through his life how God looks at human beings, at the world, at plants, at animals and at creation as a whole. Jesus revealed God as a father who goes after each one of us with loving concern and care (Lk 15), who cares for the birds in the skies and even the grass in the field (Mt 6:24-35), who embraces the "little ones" and identifies himself with them (Mk 10:13-16).

To believe means, therefore, to have a different, but ultimately the only correct view of reality. One who looks at the world with the eyes of faith does not see less but more. Faith is not a distortion of reality; it puts things in the right perspective. It lets me see the connections which exist between things and enables me to see the ultimate ground of all reality. It shows me where this turbulent and seemingly directionless world is moving. It enables me to hold on to the claim of the Bible that the jigsaw puzzle which we call history and creation can be put together into a beautiful design even if many pieces do not fit together at all in the present state of things.

2. TO BELIEVE MEANS NOT TO SEE BUT TO TRUST

To believe means to surrender oneself to a person, to let oneself be taken by the hand and to be led by that person through darkness and often through territories without roads and directions. It means to trust this person and to let him take the lead.

In the fourth watch of the night Jesus went towards them walking on the lake, and when his disciples saw him walking on the lake they were terrified. 'It is a ghost', they said, and cried out in fear. But at once Jesus called out to them, saying, 'Courage! It is I! Do not be afraid.' It was Peter who answered. 'Lord' he said 'if it is you, tell me to come to you across the water.' 'Come' said Jesus. Then Peter got out of the boat and started walking towards Jesus across the water, but as soon as he felt the force of the wind, he took fright and began to sink. 'Lord! Save me!, he cried. Jesus put out his hand at once and held him. 'Man of little faith,' he said 'why did you doubt?' And as they got into the boat the wind dropped (Mt 14: 25-33).

Faith means ultimately that I entrust myself totally to the God whom Jesus proclaimed as loving Father and finding in this love my security, my certainty and my fulfillment as person.

No one can go through this world without ever having experienced the darkness of faith and the necessity of trusting without seeing. Abraham remains the father of faith for us. He will always be the example of what faith in the biblical sense means (Heb 11:1-29). He was a man who left everything and went on an unknown journey, trusting in the one who had asked him to do so. He was ready to sacrifice even all the hope he had in his son if God demanded it. Yet he kept on trusting that this God would not let him down, even though everything seemed to be lost when God demanded the almost impossible from him by asking for the life of his son (Gn 22:1-18).

Scripture presents us with two common experiences of people who have encountered God and who have entrusted themselves to his care. On the one hand, there is the joy and security God's presence in their life gives them. On the other hand, there is the agony of a sin-permeated world in which God seemingly does not exist. His apparent absence causes so much anxiety, suffering and sometimes insult, particularly for those who have put their trust in Yahweh. The Psalms are a perfect reflection of such a situation. They must be understood as a reaction of human beings to God's prior action. It is as if God touches a human being with the intention of befriending him or her and the person reacts to this touch.

The reaction is a twofold one. The first is that of joy, of delight, of being overwhelmed by God's care and love. This reaction expresses itself in thanksgiving, adoration and praise, in songs and hymns. Many Psalms give witness to this.

The second reaction to God's touch can be a very painful one. The person reacts in pain to the experience of suffering, natural catastrophe, to God's absence, his seeming indifference, his unfairness and injustice to the ones who have put all their trust in him.

No one is spared having such an experience at times. How many saints have suffered from the experience of God's absence in their lives and in the world? They have understood what these "Psalms of Lament" were all about. Therese of Lisieux was one of those saints, who in spite of all her childlike trust and love of God, experienced God's absence intensely. She belongs to those saints who anticipated the crisis of faith that plagues so many of us today. Her greatness consists precisely in her ability to suffer and to hold on to her faith in utter darkness, while feeling abandoned and in the midst of serious doubts about God's existence right up to her death.

This saint was assaulted with terrible doubts and uncertainties concerning her faith during the last years of her religious life. It is said that she died with all these doubts and anxieties. Yet the Church proclaimed her the patroness of the missions, she identified herself with all those who find it difficult to believe.

In this saint and in the lives of many what Jesus himself had to go through is repeated. He was not spared this painful experience of human existence. According to Mark's gospel, Jesus died with a cry of desolation, feeling abandoned by his Father who meant everything to him, "My God, my God, why have you deserted me?" (Mk 15:34) And yet according to Luke, Jesus died with the words, "Father into your hands I commit my spirit" (Lk 23:46).

Anyone who opts for a faith-existence will have both experiences. At times he or she will feel the presence of God in his or her life, a presence which gives true joy and happiness. But there will be times when everything will seem so dark and incomprehensible that it will become difficult to hold on in faith to a God who claims that he loves every human being with unconditional love. This is part of human experience.

No saint has been spared such an experience. Look at that great missionary, Francis Xavier. He was convinced that only those would be saved who were baptized. Since he regarded non-Christian religions as the devil's work, he believed that anyone who wanted to become a Christian had to leave his own religion behind. He proclaimed the Word of God in Latin, believing that the proclamation itself was sufficient to lead to conversion. He also had his dark night of faith when he was close to despair and resignation. He wrote, "Once the dangers are close and one feels the loss of one's life at hand, then, in spite of all resolutions, at a sudden everything turns terrifyingly dark." The greatness of this saint consists precisely in that he was able to discover in all this darkness the cross of Christ, and to find in it the strength not to give in to what he felt.

The saints distinguish themselves from the rest of humankind in that, in spite of all disappointments, frustrations, loneliness, doubts, darkness and sufferings they did not give in to bitterness and despair. They became men and women of great kindness, compassion, and love for God and their fellow human beings. In an old book I once found this advice for priests and religious: "Make sure you reach fifty years or more, because then you will be able to radiate God's kindness and compassion to all the people you serve. Only after many years of friendship with the Lord, after many trials, sufferings and darkness which you endure in fidelity and love to your master will you be able to gain such virtues." I regard it as one of the greatest tragedies when the life of a religious or a priest or a lay person ends up in bitterness and frustration. And how often this happens!

Look also at John the Baptist, whose whole life was lived according to the principle: "I must decrease, he must increase." But before dealing with this "greatest of all born of woman", I would like to share an experience I had some years ago. It gave me a new insight into what in the end was the true cause of the saint's greatness.

In Asia I once met an old missionary who complained bitterly to me about what was happening to what he had faithfully built up in almost fifty years of dedicated work. All that he had done, all he had believed in, was questioned by the younger missionaries. Even his bishop had told him that his methods of pastoral care were outdated and misdirected. All this came close to breaking the old man's heart. I tried to explain to him that he was too pessimistic in evaluating what was a new situation. Most of what he had done produced results, but the emphasis had shifted. I added that we often needed time to see the Lord's hand in all that happens to us. He listened patiently and then he remarked, "Maybe I am like John the Baptist. He also found it so difficult to accept the way in which Christ was taking over, although he had proclaimed himself to be the one who would prepare the way for Christ."

If we look at the life of the Baptist again, we find a pattern that seems to repeat itself in the lives of those who want to follow the Lord and proclaim the

Kingdom. John was a great saint, a renowned preacher, who attracted all kinds of people, including those from the highest class of society. He was successful for quite a while (Jn 1:19-36; 3:22-34). He had many disciples, and, as we know, his movement lasted well beyond his death, as we find related in Acts (Ac 19:1-4).

The beautiful scene in the Gospel where he advises his disciples that it is time now to leave him and follow the man from Nazareth is the turning point in his life. From that moment on the spotlight shifts away from him. He is arrested and thrown into prison. Here he faces the real crisis of his life, the 'dark night of his soul'. "Are you the one to come or was I wrong?" (Mt 11:1-19). We do not know what went on in John's heart and soul. He had to realize that God's coming was happening in a way different from the way he had expected. It came in a form that was hard for him to take. Not judgement, but salvation for all.

We, like John the Baptist, are always only those who prepare the way of the Lord. We constantly tell that to the people we serve, and we believe that we are in fact only his forerunners, though at times we may act as if we are very sure of the way the Lord makes himself present and how his Kingdom has to be promoted. Yet when things turn out to be different, when God does not follow the road we thought he ought to, when our approaches are questioned, when our views are disregarded and the things we worked for and in which we invested our lives are regarded as useless and wasted, what then?

Perhaps that is the time to listen to the Baptist again and to take his advice, "Francis or Teresa, you are not the Messiah, you must decrease so that he will increase; you are not the bridegroom, you are only the friend of the bridegroom." God's ways are not our ways, and his coming is always different from what we think it should be. We are asked to follow his way and not to show him the way. At such times the Baptist may be the best saint to pray to especially for understanding.

3. TO BELIEVE MEANS TO BE ON GUARD NOT TO LOSE THE TREASURE

The last petition in the "Our Father" reads, "And lead us not into temptation but deliver us from evil." What is this temptation? The disciple who lives in the end-time and who has sided with Jesus in the great eschatological battle, will have to experience the force of the "final assault". The temptation for the apostle is apostasy, or falling away. More precisely, it is the constant temptation to lose faith that the Kingdom is already in the world; it is the temptation to regard the experience of the Kingdom present in our world as an illusion; to give in to despair. It means to give up believing that the Kingdom which is present only in the form of a tiny seed (Mt 13:31ff) will ultimately grow into a large tree. It is the ever-present temptation to lose hope that God can bring about a glorious end out of the small beginning we experience in the present.

This "apostasy" does not have to be a dramatic event. It is a temptation to which we can all easily succumb without even realizing it. It is often a gradual process. It is the temptation to give in to doubts and finally to give in to frustration, bitterness and despair. In short, we lose our faith that God's Kingdom is already in this world and that he will lead this world to its final destiny - the fullness of the Kingdom. The danger of losing one's faith is a constant one, since we are always exposed to frustrations, loneliness, doubts and delusions, - which can easily lead to bitterness and despair. Jesus knew why he included this petition in the disciples' prayer. In this last petition he warns us against any false enthusiasm, "Remember, you are engaged in the eschatological battle, watch out!" We pray, "Dear Father, this one request grant us — preserve us from falling away from Thee." St Paul tells us that we carry this treasure in earthen vessels (2 Cor 4:7) We can preserve this treasure only if we constantly rediscover and cherish it.

We find the same concern in many Psalms, which are a cry not to be tested beyond our strength. We have to remind ourselves again and again of God's presence and care in our life as we find it so beautifully expressed in Psalm 23, "The Lord is my shepherd." This Psalm has been a comfort and strength for millions of people who found themselves walking in the valley of darkness and who cried out to God for guidance and protection. Dietrich Bonhoeffer, who was imprisoned by the Nazis and subsequently hanged, found in this Psalm the strength and the courage to face the horrors of the concentration camp and, finally, death itself.

An experience I had years ago gave this Psalm a special meaning in my life. I was doing some work in Baltimore. I came to know a man who was totally paralyzed. He was forty years old, and his health was such that, despite his paralysis he could have gone on living indefinitely. One day I asked him, "How do you cope with the prospect that you could be living this way of life for forty or fifty years more?" He answered me, "Yes Father, you are right. There are moments when I am close to despair. But I found a secret that works for me every day. Every morning when I wake up my first prayer are the words of Psalm 23, 'The Lord is my shepherd.' This prayer at least gives me the strength to get through the day. Every day it has the same effect on me. It fills me with the certainty that God cares for me and that my suffering is not forgotten. The Lord seems to know why I should live this way."

4. TO BELIEVE MEANS TO BE CONSTANTLY DIRECTED TO-WARD THE FUTURE COMING OF THE LORD

A believer lives in an attitude of provisionality in that he or she regards this life as a dim anticipation of what is to come. It makes him or her like an outstretched finger towards the future. It is not as if a believer does not take this world seriously; he or she takes it more seriously than a non-believer, since in faith they know that it is this world which will be transformed into the New Heaven and the New Earth. Yet the believer also knows very well that this world is not the fulfillment of what God has in store for us. Therefore, one looks towards the future in hope and anticipation. One cannot live this life of faith without this constant orientation towards "the day of the Lord." Like the wise virgins, we are people who should "yearn" for the coming of the Kingdom in its fullness. Our prayers should always end with the cry: "Come Lord Jesus!"

J.B.Metz in his book, FOLLOWERS OF CHRIST asks the question: "Why does the Lord not come? Maybe we don't want him to come? We do not really yearn for his coming although our very existence is a cry for that final fulfillment." We do pray in each Eucharist, "We await his coming in glory", but how real is our waiting? Particularly those who have vowed to live a life of celibacy are by their very existence as celibates "signs of the provisionality of the present" and a firm reminder of all Christian hope — the fullness of the Kingdom still to come. But are we really expecting the "New Heaven and New Earth"?

> We are people who cannot settle for what is. We hope and firmly believe in the "New Heaven and the New Earth." We await that re-creation as God's greatest gift to all human beings, towards which the whole of creation groans in agony and waits in hope that it may participate in our glory and find its own fulfillment as well (Rm 8:22-23).

> Our faith is a journey, and anyone on a long journey wants to get home.

Questions for Reflection:

1. How strong is my belief that this sin-permeated world is held in the hands of a God who loves me and everybody unconditionally?

2. What are the obstacles in my life that assault my faith to believe in a loving and caring God?

3. What Scripture texts or prayers give me comfort and strength when I feel I am "walking in the valley of darkness" and I am inclined to give in to bitterness or despair?

Story for Reflection:

Faith is a risk. Do I dare to launch out into the unknown and to trust this inner instinct that I am called to more than the mediocre state of a half-committed Christian? Like the migrant bird in this story I am faced with a decision if I want to live my faith to the full.

THE TINY BIRDS

Migration is not an easy or a pleasant thing for a tiny bird to face. It must turn deliberately from solid land, from food, shelter, and a certain measure of security, and fly across an ocean unfriendly to its life, destitute of everything it needs. We make much of the heroism and endurance of our airmen and explorers. Perhaps some day, a man will rival the adventurous hope of the willow wren and the chiffchaff; an ounce and a half of living courage, launching out with amazing confidence to a prospect of storms, hardship, exhaustion — perhaps starvation and death. Careful minds would hardly think the risk worth taking. But the tiny bird, before conditions force it — not driven by fear, but drawn by Hope — commits itself with perfect confidence to that infinite ocean of air, where all familiar landmarks will vanish, and where, if its strength fails, it must be lost. And the bird's hope is justified. There IS summer at the other end of the perilous journey. The scrap of valiant life obeys a true instinct when it launches itself into the air. It is urged from within towards a goal it can attain; and may reckon the suffering of the moment not worthy to be compared to the glory that shall be revealed.

(Evelyn Underhill)

THE KINGDOM: CALL TO FELLOWSHIP WITH CHRIST

Introduction

What is "NEW" in Jesus' message is his image of God as unconditional love. With this message Jesus set himself apart from the theology of his time. CONVERSION means I let this image of God enter my life and change my mistaken image of God. It means I start looking at myself, my friends, my Church and society, at nature and climate from a different point of view. I start loving them not with my own love but with the love of God for me. I start thinking and acting as Jesus did, in short, I follow him. Conversion leads to fellowship.

Perhaps one of the most powerful examples of what it means to love with the love of Christ was given to me by a woman who was married to an impossible husband.

He was a hopeless drunkard, often unfaithful and his behavior towards his wife was at times unbearable. She had a thousand reasons for divorce. I asked her one day, how she could continue to live with this man. Her answer was, "Well Father, I could not do so if I had not myself experienced that the Lord loves my husband. It was He who taught me to love him and showed me that my husband needed my love. That I can do this at all is a gift from him. It is the Lord's love for my husband that is at work here and not just my natural capacity to offer it."

Discipleship is the basic theme of all the Gospels. Jesus spent most of his time during his public ministry with his disciples and he led them gradually to his way of thinking, feeling, judging and acting. There are hundreds of texts in Scripture which refer to fellowship. The words disciple and fellowship occur 250 times in the New Testament. I would like to concentrate on one text which tells us something essential about discipleship — Mk 3:13-15. In this text on the election of the twelve apostles we find the most significant elements that pertain to discipleship as Jesus himself understood it.

I HAVE CHOSEN YOU
TO BE WITH ME AND
TO BE SENT OUT

I would like to use this text, therefore, to concentrate on these three basic elements that reveal to us the true meaning of discipleship as Jesus saw it.

1. I CHOSE YOU, YOU DID NOT CHOOSE ME (Jn 15:16)

The simple request of Jesus, "Follow me," always comes as a surprise. It is always a question of a basic choice, of a turning point in Life. Jesus presents himself as an absolute value to which everything has to be subordinated. How can Jesus ask for such a commitment? In the Bible this call is answered by many with immediate obedience (Mt 9:9). Why? Is there an affinity, a liking or a fanaticism involved? Why do the disciples follow Jesus? What are they looking for? What do they find?

Jesus himself is the protagonist of real discipleship. His life is ruled by a constant attitude of availability to the Father. His life-motto is, "I always do what pleases him" (Jn 8:29; 14:31) — to do the will of his Father, who has sent him, and to bring his work to completion is his food (Jn 4:31-34). Jesus is the first to practice discipleship, which he then demands from those who follow him. In order to please the Father, the disciple will have to follow Jesus. The terms "to follow, to imitate, to obey, to dedicate" come from the desert experience when the people "followed Yahweh" who in the "pillar of fire or in the cloud" determined the direction the people would take. "To follow Yahweh" was the cause of the very life of Israel. Jesus demands that he is to be followed as Yahweh was followed. The absoluteness of Jesus' call rests on the perception that it is God himself who calls one to fellowship. Jesus always regards his disciples as a gift from the Father. Not he, but the Father has called them to follow him. Jesus, therefore, loves and treasures them because they belong to the Father and he has received them from the Father.

I have made your name known to the men you took from the world to give me. They were yours and you gave them to me (Jn 17:6; 6:44; 10:29).

The reason why Jesus can demand such fellowship with him seems to be that God the Father is demanding such following since he gives the vocation and presents Jesus as an absolute value to which everything has to be subordinated. To obey Jesus means to obey the Father who calls.

At times it is worth meditating on how we received our vocation or particular calling in order to understand that it is a concrete realization of God's unconditional love for us. But why did he choose me? There is no answer except the one already given in the Old Testament:

> If Yahweh set his heart on you and chose you, it was not because you outnumbered other peoples...It was for love of you (Dt 7:7).

> No one can come to me unless the Father draws him (Jn 6:65).

At times, when I look at the people whom the good Lord has chosen, I am tempted to ask, "My God, could you not find better disciples?" The Lord would most probably answer, "I did not choose you because you were more virtuous or pious, more handsome or beautiful, no, I chose you because I loved you". A mystic once said, "God loves every human being unconditionally but he chooses some to reach others". The basis of my vocation is God's preferential love for me. On this love I can and must rely. There are three elements in each vocation on which we should reflect

1. There is a **WITNESS** who directs us to Jesus. This witness is like John the Baptist, who pointed to Jesus. If you look back on your vocation or calling, you should be able to discern who directed you to Christ, saying, "This is the Lamb of God, follow him" (Jn 1:36). Perhaps it was the quiet witness of a parent, a grandparent, a friend, a priest or sister who just by his of her very life was like the outstretched finger of the Baptist telling you, "If you want a truly fulfilled and challenging life, follow him".

2. There is a **VISION**. It might have been the dream of a personal fulfillment in life that would take you far beyond mere human fulfillment. If this vision dies, it is hard to go on. To have a vision for oneself and for the group to which one belongs is essential for all renewal. It is interesting to observe that those congregations with a clear vision are those which prosper most, for example, the community of Mother Teresa, or that of the Little Brothers and Sisters of Charles de Foucauld, or Taize.

The vision we had at the beginning of our vocation is very important for the rest of our life. When the risen Lord appeared at Easter to Mary Magdalene he told her, "Tell my disciples to go back to Galilee" (Mk 16:7). Why to Galilee? It was there they had received their first vision, where the spring of their vocation had been lived, where their youthful enthusiasm had blossomed, where they had seen who the Lord was. After the crucifixion of the Lord their vision was destroyed. Where should they start again? Jesus tells them, "Go back to Galilee, remember your first vision, the spring of your vocation when I called you. Let this vision surface again and then listen to what the witnesses of the resurrection tell you and you will understand. So it very often is with us. We have to go back to where it all started, to the vision that was there in the beginning when the Lord said, "Come follow me" (Mk 1: 16-20). This is our treasure and we need to unearth it.

> When a disciple came from a far-away country, the Master asked,
> "What are you seeking?"
> "Enlightenment."
> "You have your own treasure house. Why do you search outside?"
> "Where is my treasure house?"
> "This seeking that has come upon you."
> At that moment the disciple was enlightened.
> Years later he would say to friends,
> "Open your own treasure house and enjoy your treasures."
>   (A.de Mello, *One Minute Wisdom*)

If the vision dies it is very difficult to go on. When someone asked me, as director of a twenty-week renewal course for priests and religious, what we would like to achieve in these twenty weeks, I used to say," All we want is to let the vision the men had when they began their priestly or religious life arise anew, to make it become bright once again." If we can do that, the course will have been very good. As Nietzsche put it,"He who has a WHY to live for will always find a HOW". Of course, every vision undergoes changes, since it is a living reality. We need new motivations and a constant deepening of our vision if we want it to stay alive and remain the guiding star of our life. I like to ask people who once had a very vivid experience of their vocation, if they have remained faithful to what they saw. The amazing thing is that one can really revive a vision and make it shine again in all its attractive beauty.

3. There is a **CALL**. At times it is hard to say when it all happened. Yet a personal experience of being called in one way or the other seems to be very important in any vocation. Without it, it might be difficult to survive. For many what T.S. Eliot said might be true: "We had the experience but we missed the meaning." Each of us in our commitment to the Lord will be led into life situations and crises where there seems to be nothing left to rely on — no friends, no enthusiasm of others, no inspiring book, no renewal course or excellent talks. Nothing seems to remove the doubts and darkness. Only the personal experience

of my calling that came to me when Christ said to me personally, "Come follow me," will enable me to bear the doubts and the darkness and to go on relying on what I have seen in the past. In such moments I will have to go back to Galilee, like the apostles whom the risen Lord directed to return to the place of their first encounter with him (Mk 16:7). There they would recover their vocation and call which had been badly shaken by the crucifixion and death of their master. Anyone who has no Galilee to go back to, that is, one who has never experienced a personal encounter with the Lord, will have nothing on which to rely when the crises come.

To illustrate the point: During the time of the desert monks, around 450 A.D., a young monk went to an old and holy monk and asked him, "Father, how is it that so many today leave the monastery? The old man answered him, "When a good hunting dog sees a rabbit, he will immediately run after it, howling and barking with excitement. This will, of course, attract other dogs, and they in turn will run and bark and howl like the one that saw the rabbit, although they have not actually seen it themselves. After a while the ones who did not really see the rabbit, but relied only on the barking and howling of the first dog, will get tired and give up the chase, because they are no longer interested. They drift off and go home. Only the dog that really saw the rabbit will go on running and eventually catch up with it. That is the way with many who enter," the old monk concluded. "Only the one who has his or her eyes on Christ and has seen him will and can survive. The others, who came only because the enthusiasm of others had drawn them will lose interest and leave."

Reflect on the three elements of your vocation.

WITNESS: Do you pray with gratitude for those who
    directed you to Jesus?

VISION: What was the vision which attracted you
    to follow the Lord?

CALL: What personal experience of Jesus have you had
    in the past? Today?

2. TO STAY WITH ME

To stay with Jesus seems to be the most essential element of discipleship. Once the first step is taken, once the disciple has gone with the Lord in order to "see where he lives" (Jn 1:39) what happens then? What changes take place in the life of the disciple?

a. A relationship of special intimacy and familiarity begins to emerge.

The disciple is called to grow into friendship with the Lord. He is urged to form a community of life with the Lord. This aspect is particularly well expressed in the Gospel of John. In the first vocation story (Jn 1:39), Jesus invites his disciples by saying, "Come, experience for yourself." John adds, "..they stayed where he stayed." The wording is very carefully chosen: They stayed with the Lord or remained with him.

John regards this abiding or remaining with the Lord as the climax of the disciple's growth in fellowship with him. Yet he makes a subtle distinction. At the beginning of the Gospel John says, "They remained WITH him"(1:39). However, at the end of the Gospel, after the disciples had stayed with the Lord, Jesus asks them to "remain IN him" (Jn 15:14). Indwelling is the goal of all discipleship. John insists that the disciple must grow from what he has heard about the Lord, from what might have drawn him into the company of the disciples to a personal experience of the Lord. If this does not happen, the disciple will always be looking for more knowledge, for more information, for the latest theology, but never really get to know Christ. Then the Gospel will remain only a "worldview" but never become a way of life.

Jesus' whole mission consisted in making us his friends by drawing us into his life to the point where he can say, "You are my friends because I have made known to you everything I have learnt from my Father" (Jn 15:15). He asked his friends "To make their homes in him as he makes his home in them" (Jn 15:4-5). A similar view we find in St. Paul. He saw the purpose of his mission to the nations as: "that Christ may make his home in their hearts."

b. The disciple begins to act and to behave as Jesus does.

There are steps in this process. Living with the Lord and following him, the disciple gradually learns to think and to evaluate as Jesus does; he or she begins to see with the eyes of the Master, to learn from Jesus' own behavior and practice. As he or she sees how Jesus cares, shows compassion and understanding, how he cures, and forgives, the disciple begins to participate in these feelings, this kindness, this compassion. The action of the master begins to mold the disciple from the inside. As he sees Jesus praying he asks him to teach him to pray (Lk 11:1) and to introduce him to a prayer-life like his own.

c.To be a disciple is not an individual adventure, it means joining a group.

When Jesus calls someone he does not go with him into the mountains or the desert and gives the person a personal introduction to his new way of life. He just tells him or her, "Join the group, stay with them." As a member of the group the disciple learns what it means to follow the Master. Since the disciples are not perfect, but ordinary human beings with all the ambitions of ordinary people, tensions arise among them. Some ask for the first places (Mk 10:38), but Jesus takes them as they are. He does not expect them to be perfect. Together in trial and error they come to realize what it means to follow the Master and to adopt the behavior Jesus asks of them: to drop behind him, to be ready to go the way of the cross as he does, to write themselves off in terms of any kind of importance, privilege or right and to spend their time only in the service of others. Mark 8:26-10:45 presents what it means to be a disciple in the eyes of Jesus.

Discipleship is a long process that involves the whole person and most probably will take a lifetime. It might be interesting to note that the Puebla Conference, which was so much concerned with the Church's social involvement, mentions as the prime priority for a fruitful religious life a deep experience of the Lord (726).

There can be no convincing and persevering evangelization without a constant contact with the Lord.

3. TO BE SENT OUT: "AS THE FATHER HAS SENT ME SO I AM SENDING YOU" (Jn 20:21)

The heart of all apostolic activity is that we are shaped and formed by our being with the Lord. The prerequisite for any kind of fruitful apostolate is the constant experience of a personal relationship with Christ, a long familiarity with him. What we are to preach is our friendship with Christ. Like St. John, who communicated only what he had seen, touched and lived with (1 Jn 1:1-4) so also we can only communicate what we ourselves have experienced first.

What we have seen with our own eyes, what we have heard with our own ears, what our hands have touched, that we communicate to you so that you will join with us in the fellowship that we have with the Father and with the Son Jesus Christ.

The realization that what people want is the witness of our lives was brought home to me very forcefully during an international conference on Religious experience in Hinduism and Christianity.

During a discussion a Hindu theologian said to me rather emphatically, "Father, please don't just quote your scriptures to me. I have read the Bible several times and studied it thoroughly. I believe that I know it better than many Christians. All I ask is that you tell me how you personally experience your God in Jesus Christ and I will tell you how I experience my God. Dialogue, after all means exchange of experience."

The advantage of the disciple is not that he has to know the latest in theology and the most advanced means of communication but that he has "been with the Lord". This is beautifully explained in the testimony the Jerusalem Council gave concerning Peter and John:

When the Council saw the boldness of Peter and John and could see that they were obviously uneducated non-professionals, they were amazed, and realized what being with Jesus had done for them (Ac 4:13).

Jesus entrusted his mission, his own ministry to his disciples. They were to be his representatives through the centuries to come."As the Father has sent me, so I am sending you" (Jn 20:21).

What ministry did Jesus come to fulfill and expects us to carry on? If by ministry we mean a service performed in response to the human needs of people, we might ask: WHAT NEED DID JESUS COME TO FULFILL?

One could say Jesus came to serve the ultimate need of any human person, the need for redemption and salvation. He came to fulfill the ultimate longing of any human heart, to find a resting place in union and communion with God.

Restless is our heart, O God, until it rests in you. (St. Augustine)

A person's ultimate aim is the realization of God. I live and move and have my being in pursuit of this goal. (M. Ghandi)

How Did Jesus Fulfill This Ministry?

He revealed to us that God has created every human being in his own image and likeness and that in order to achieve final salvation this likeness of God must come to completion in every human person. The power to transform us from mere image to likeness is God's infinite love for us. This is the love Jesus proclaims as present in him and available to us through him. This presence of God in the world as transforming love is the ultimate reality that lies behind all reality and ultimately behind all human needs.

St. Paul summarizes this mystery of God's love for every human person in the words, "Christ lives in you, the hope of a glory to come" (Col 1:24-27). Our call is to give expression to this truth in all our life, in all our words, in all our actions and in all our relationships.

The fundamental condition for preaching the Good News is that we ourselves are filled with this experience. We can only communicate what we are experiencing ourselves. Practically, this means that to be a disciple of Jesus I must have an ongoing life of intimacy with the Lord. I must deliberately bring my own faith experience that "Christ lives in me" to conscious awareness. My being sent by the Lord means then to minister this Good News to all people, to help them to discover the Christ image in the depth of their very being and to bring this image to perfection in them. This truth was brought home to me once by an African artist whom I visited in his little studio.

The statue fascinated me. It was made out of ebony, black and beautifully carved with sensuous lines and a texture that conveyed a deep spiritual element. I wanted to buy it, but the missionary did not want to part with it. It had been a gift to him. He promised to bring me to the man who carved it. Maybe he had another one he might sell. The next day I met him in his little hut. He was rather young, shy, and as black as the wood he was working on. He showed me a few of his works. Among them was a statue of the Blessed Mother. I found it to be the most beautiful I had ever seen. I asked him in amazement, "How do you do it? How do you picture these images and then carve them into wood?" His answer was as simple as he was, "Oh no, Father, I don't carve these images into the wood, the images are in the wood. I see them there and they just plead to be brought out and set free."

Our mission is to make people aware of this marvelous reality that Christ lives already in them. This image of Christ pleads to be carved out, to be made visible. God wants us to be transformed into the image of his beloved Son. Only so can we truly become what God has put into each one of us: His own image. We must open ourselves to this reality within us and let it take over our entire lives.

As a disciple of Jesus in whom Christ is present the question is: Am I able to see the 'face in the wood', the image of Christ in the often formless and ugly shape of people? And when I have seen the image of Christ in my fellow human beings, am I willing to make this image visible? To be a minister means first to SEE and then to go and make VISIBLE what I saw.

However, in our contact with people we should not forget that God's love always makes itself present in "concrete shapes". The services we perform to meet the needs of others are the concrete shapes through which God's love reaches people. Only through us can his love be made present and real to people, as the following story so clearly demonstrates:

One morning Mother Teresa noticed a gathering of people outside the Kali temple. As she drew near to them she saw a man stretched out on the ground with upturned eyes and a face apparently drained of blood. A triple cord denoted that he was a Brahmin, one of the priests from the temple. No one dared to touch him. They knew he was suffering from cholera. She bent over, took the body of the Brahmin in her arms, and carried him to the home for the dying. Day and night she nursed him, and eventually he recovered. One day he was to explain. "For thirty years I have worshipped a Kali of stone. But here is the real Kali, a Kali of flesh and blood." (D. Lapierre, *City of Joy*)

How much people really need and look for this primary witness of our evangelizing was brought home to me in the following experiences:

After a retreat in Africa I was invited to participate in a celebration at the occasion of the inauguration of an irrigation project. It had been built through the enormous effort and commitment of the missionaries working there. Around 5000 people took part in a characteristically African way of celebration. Every village chief gave his speech. They all lauded the missionaries, the bishop and the benefactors who had helped to make the project possible. They listed all the benefits it would have for them and their children. Finally the paramount chief of the area was asked to give the last words. He was known for his deep wisdom and great leadership. He himself was not a Christian but held on to his ancestral faith. When he stood up all fell quiet immediately, so not to miss his words. His speech was remarkably brief. He said, "Bishop, we really are grateful for what these missionaries have done. We appreciate their presence and work that went into realizing this project. It is a great boon for my people. But now that we have the cooperatives and the irrigation system in place, would you please send us a few priests and sisters who can share with us their experience of God, and how this has changed their lives."

The chief had certainly no intention to offend anyone. The missionaries had not been mere development workers. Still, it made me think how important it is that we do not overlook in all our works for others that we are called ultimately to serve the deepest need of every human being — the unfolding of the 'hidden self' that only takes place when one is led to a personal encounter with Christ.

I have known many selfless young people who were deeply involved in the social apostolate and who told me that they could not keep on witnessing to the Kingdom of justice and peace the way Jesus understood it, without being in constant close contact with HIM. What saved them from dropping out of this difficult work was prayer and time to discern and to concentrate once again on the Lord alone. To be able to serve others selflessly and to see Christ alive in them is possible only if we ourselves stay close to Christ.

The image of the artist carving out of the wood the beautiful face of a person offers us a fine illustration of the relationship between contemplation and ministry. To contemplate is to see, and to minister is to make visible; the contemplative life is a life of vision, and the life of ministry is a life in which this vision is revealed to others.

I might quote once again the example of Mother Teresa who, more than anyone today, demonstrates what genuine following of Christ means in the setting of our work. Her famous phrase, which sums up her whole spirituality, is well known:

When I adore the eucharistic Christ I see my poor people. When I serve my poor brothers and sisters, I see Christ.

To experience Christ and to be able to discover him in others, I must spend time with the Lord in adoration and contemplation and I must serve in "concrete shape" my brothers and sisters.

Questions for Reflection:

1. How far do I realize that God's love made present and real in this world depends on my commitment to this love, that I am all he has?

2. Are all the services which I render to others, in the last analysis, aimed at serving their ultimate need, which is - to come to know God's unconditional love for them?

3. Can I say that my apostolate consists in communicating to people my own experience of Christ?

THIS JESUS CHALLENGES ME

I am FURIOUS, and he tells me: FORGIVE!
I am AFRAID, and he tells me: TAKE COURAGE!
I have DOUBTS, and he says to me: HAVE CONFIDENCE!
I feel RESTLESS, and he says to me: BE CALM!

I prefer to go MY OWN WAY, and he tells me: COME AND FOLLOW ME!
I make MY OWN PLANS, and he says to me: FORGET ABOUT THEM!
I aim towards MATERIAL GOODS, and he says: LEAVE THEM BEHIND!
I want SECURITY, and he says: I PROMISE YOU ABSOLUTELY NOTHING!

I like to live MY OWN LIFE, and he says: LOSE YOUR LIFE!
I believe I AM GOOD, and he tells me: GOOD IS NOT SUFFICIENT!
I like to BE THE BOSS, and he says: SERVE!
I like to COMMAND OTHERS, and he says: OBEY!

I like to UNDERSTAND, and he says: BELIEVE!
I like CLARITY, and he speaks to me in PARABLES.
I like POETRY, and he speaks to me in REALITIES.
I like my TRANQUILITY, and he likes me to be DISTURBED.

I like VIOLENCE, and he says: PEACE BE WITH YOU!
I draw the SWORD, and he says: PUT THAT AWAY!
I think of REVENGE, and he says: OFFER THE OTHER CHEEK!
I speak of ORDER, and he says: I HAVE COME TO BRING THE SWORD!
I choose HATRED, and he says: LOVE YOUR ENEMIES.

I try to sow HARMONY, and he says:
    I HAVE COME TO CAST FIRE UPON THE EARTH!
I like to be the GREATEST, and he says:
    LEARN TO BE AS SMALL AS A CHILD!

I like to remain HIDDEN, and he says:
    LET YOUR LIGHT SHINE!
I look at the BEST PLACE, and he says:
    SIT IN THE LAST BENCH!
I like to be NOTICED, and he says:
    PRAY IN YOUR ROOM BEHIND LOCKED DOORS!

No, I don't understand this Jesus.
He provokes me. He confuses me.
Like so many of his disciples
I, too, would like to follow another Master
who would be more certain and less demanding.

But I experienced almost the same as Peter:
"I do not know of anyone else,
WHO HAS THE WORDS OF ETERNAL LIFE!"

                (Pe. Zezinho, SCJ, Brazil)

CHOSEN AGAIN: SECOND CALLING

Introduction

Scholars have persistently indicated that there are two phases concerning the call to discipleship as it is portrayed in the Gospel: the GALILEAN PHASE and DISCIPLESHIP to JERUSALEM.(The second is the more decisive). Here fellowship means to follow Jesus to Jerusalem with the prospect of sharing in his Paschal Mystery. Everyone who seriously wants to follow the Lord will have to pass through these phases in one way or the other. It is here that spiritual writers today speak about second conversion or a "qualitative change" in one's spiritual life. For many this may be a very gradual development in their spiritual life but for some it can show itself in a painful and often dramatic or even tragic happening in their lives.

What is a second conversion? This question can best be answered with a concrete example Scripture offers us: the vocation story of Peter, the apostle. The same process of growth to mature discipleship is evident in the lives of the other apostles like James and John and Paul, as well, although it is not as dramatic a process as is it with Peter.

1: THE VOCATION STORY OF SAINT PETER

The Galilean phase of his vocation

The vocation story of Peter comes to its first conclusion with the miraculous catch of fish as Luke portrays it in chapter 5 of his Gospel. Peter might have been listening to Jesus for some time without feeling called to a more radical way of following him. The miracle of the draught of fishes convinced Peter that here was more than just a wise preacher. He seemingly now makes his total commitment to the Lord. The sign of his conversion and that of his companions is that "they left all and followed Jesus" (Lk 5:11). When we look a little more closely at the actual 'living out' of this commitment he made so generously after the catch of fish, we see that this was only the beginning of a long process. Peter shows a great deal of generosity, enthusiasm, impulsiveness, good will, and a great feeling of genuine love for his Master. But we also see an excessive confidence in his own capabilities. His idea about the Kingdom and Christ's mission remain quite superficial, and when Jesus starts talking about the cross as part of his mission and as part of discipleship Peter is shocked.

Jesus had taken a lot of pains to introduce his followers gradually into his own ministry. Although he always takes them as they are, at times he does get impatient with them. Seventeen times we hear the subtle reproach, "Are your minds so dull; don't you understand; are you still without comprehension"? (Mk 8:17-18; Mt 16:8-9; Lk 9:41).

Of great significance is the famous Galilean scene where Jesus asks that decisive question, "WHO DO YOU SAY I AM ?"(Mk 8:28). This is an important moment in the disciples' lives with the Master. Jesus puts them to a test to see how far they had grasped and understood him and his mission after living with him for almost three years, during which he had tried to introduce them patiently into the mystery of his person and mission. It is Peter, the spokesman for them all who surprisingly reveals specific depth of understanding as to who Jesus is, "You are the Christ, the Son of the living God". His answer surprises even Jesus (Mt 16:17). Somehow they had understood who he was and Jesus seemed to have been successful in his effort to reveal to them the mystery of his person.

But now he wants to move them to a greater depth by making it clear to them that suffering and persecution belong to his mission and therefore to being his disciple. Here the disciples fail. This idea is utterly against their whole understanding of the Messiah who was supposed to be a glorious figure, who would restore Israel to its final glory, and who would erect such a magnificent kingdom that they themselves would fight for the first places in it (Mk 9:34; Mt 20:21). Peter's answer to Jesus' revelation that suffering is part of his mission and, therefore, of the mission of any disciple, is short but determined, "Heaven preserve you, Lord", he said, "this must not happen to you" (Mt 16:21; Mk 8:32).

Jesus' reply to Peter is hard, "If you Peter want to be my disciple then get behind me and let me determine the way. Do not tell me the way a disciple has to go." It seems that Peter does not understand. It is not only Peter who has not yet grasped Jesus' vision; the others had their own ideas about it. James and John let their mother do the lobbying for them with regard to their political position in the coming glorious Kingdom of Israel (Mt 20:20-26). When the Samaritans did not welcome them, the disciples suggest that Jesus should call fire from heaven and burn the whole place up to teach these Samaritans a lesson (Lk 9:54).

During the hour of the Passion Peter experienced in a dramatic way his limitations, as well as the precariousness of his commitment. Full of emotional fervor, he announced that he would never abandon the Master even if everyone else did, "Though all lose faith in you I will never lose faith...Even if I have to die with you, I will never disown you." Again we should not overlook that the text adds, "And all the other disciples said the same" (Mt 26:33-35). Not many hours later, Peter denied his Lord three times.

This incident gave rise to Peter's most serious vocation crisis. It made him understand how superficial his commitment had been, and all his self-sufficiency crumbles, "And he went outside and wept bitterly" (Mt 26:75). Jesus takes advantage of this very crisis to call him again to a more mature and decisive conversion. This scene takes place after the Resurrection.

2. THE SECOND CALLING OF PETER

The scene is very much like that when the first call was issued. The setting is the same, the Lake of Galilee; the circumstances similar. Peter and the other apostles are fishing and have caught nothing all night long. At daybreak, Jesus, standing on the shore, tells them to cast their nets to the right side of the boat. They do so and make an enormous catch of fish. Then they all come ashore to eat with Jesus. Only twice in the Gospels do we find "charcoal fire" mentioned: in the courtyard of the High Priest (Jn 18:18) and in the encounter of Peter with the risen Lord. "They saw a charcoal fire there" (Jn 21:9). It was at a charcoal fire that Peter denied his Master three times and it was in the presence of a charcoal fire that Peter is asked to confess his love for his Master anew. After what had happened to him in the light of charcoal fires, Peter might never have looked at them in later life without recalling painful memories.

After the meal, Jesus addresses Peter as he had some years before and calls him to follow him, this time in the form of a triple question, "Simon, do you love me more than these?"..."Yes Lord, you know that I love you"..."Feed my sheep" (Jn 21:1-19). Now Jesus asks Peter, "Do you love me more than these others do?" Why does Jesus make this comparison? It seems he is asking Peter: What is really the motivating force of your life; on what are your sights actually set? Are you still focused on yourself, on your successes and accomplishments, comparing yourself with others, relying on your own resources and powers, on your own capacity to love?

What makes the temptation of power so seemingly irresistible? Maybe it is that power offers an easy substitute for the hard task of love. It seems easier to be God than to love God, easier to control people than to love people, easier to own life than to love life. Jesus asks, "Do you love me?" We ask, "Can we sit at your right hand and your left hand in your Kingdom?" (Mt 20:21). (Henry Nouwen, *In the Name of Jesus*)

Peter had been able to overcome his crisis and to say "Yes" to Jesus, but the crisis has taught him much. It allowed him to make a more mature response, deepened, and qualitatively different from that of three years before. Now he is aware of his limits and of his faults, and this knowledge makes him more humble. Now his commitment is no longer based upon his own capabilities but rather on the word of Jesus who called him. Now he commits himself to a crucified Lord and to a Kingdom that is not of this earth and is built on faith. He is willing to follow the Lord with no illusions or sentimentalism.

To Peter, who was very much a doer and an active man, Jesus says, "My lambs and my sheep will be nourished not so much by what you, Peter, DO for them, but by the way you communicate to them my love for you and your believing love for me, by the way they can experience the reality of my presence to you and your presence to me." Obviously then, it is the communication of Jesus' loving presence that is paramount in being an apostle more than the apparent success of our ministry.

When Mother Teresa was asked how she could face the overwhelming odds against her work in Calcutta, where the people she cared for were just a tiny fraction of those dying in the streets, she replied, "It is not my job to be successful. It is my job to be faithful." Jesus seems to underscore this call to faithful love in the next part of the dialogue:

I tell you solemnly, when you were young, you put on your own belt and walked where you liked; but when you grow older you will stretch out your hands, and somebody else will put a belt around you and take you where you would rather not go. In these words he indicated the kind of death by which Peter would give glory to God. And after this he said: Follow me (Jn 21:18-19).

This was a decisive moment for Peter - a new call to die to himself in a more radical way and to choose Jesus with a vision made clearer by love — a love purified of arrogance and self-reliance. His following the Lord will be based on faith and trust in the power of Christ's love for him. Before Peter had left his boat, work, house and family in a generous gesture, but now he is asked to hand himself over to be led "where he would rather not go."

What Jesus asked of Peter he himself had to go through as well. The Gospels mention the phrase "he was handed over" twenty-two times. The basic meaning of this phrase is that in the life of Jesus there came a time when he was no longer the active subject, fully in command of all his actions, but had become the object on which others acted. Jesus himself moved from action to passion, from the role of subject to that of object, and, from working in freedom, to waiting upon what others decided and receiving what others did. At times this meant being led "where he would rather not have gone."

The ultimate goal of a disciple is not just doing what the Master did but to be led and guided by the Master's spirit.

A young man was apprenticed to a master artist who produced the most beautiful stained glass windows anywhere. The apprentice could not approach the master's genius, so he borrowed his master's tools, thinking that was the answer. After several weeks, the young man said to his teacher, "I'm not doing any better with your tools than I did with mine." The teacher replied, "So, it's not the tools of the master you need; it's the spirit of the master you are in need of."

Our Call to Mature Discipleship

Everyone who seriously follows the Lord will somehow have to travel the same road as Peter. The discipleship of Peter, from his superficial first conversion to his later mature one of faith through crisis, is a paradigm of the conversion process of every Christian. Like Peter, we at some moment of our life heard our first call to fellowship with Jesus. We decided to follow Christ with total dedication. Like the apostles we became disciples "abandoning boats and nets" and even families, which seemed to us then the height of generosity.

Discipleship was most attractive and seemed realizable. The Lord's presence was felt and prayer brought us the consolation that helped us face the difficulties of living out our apostolate in which Jesus was "felt" to be our support and inspiration. Poverty had its own aura. Celibacy, though always a renunciation of something beautiful, was a joy because of the presence of Christ and of his evangelical ideal, felt so strongly in our hearts. Even though our first years in the priesthood and in religious life were not without their struggles and difficulties, for most of us there was a generosity and fervor that enabled us to be radical.

But what has happened over the years? Gradually, almost imperceptibly, there is an ebbing away of the first enthusiasm. Somehow the goal becomes blurred, obscured. Zeal can degenerate into excessive activity. With varying degrees of consciousness, we can begin building up our own kingdom in which we become more and more entrenched as the years pass by. We may run our mission, our parish, our school, our dispensary, seminary very efficiently and successfully, but often our own projects run our lives.

> Half the time we are not choosing but drifting along on whatever current is under us, acting on impulse or routine, conforming to convention or answering expectations. (Ruth Burrows)

We easily become dispirited if our projects fail; or if there's a lack of appreciation for what we do. Perhaps the people in the community are impossible to live with. For any or all of these reasons we can begin to experience a certain loneliness, a kind of isolation, an emptiness. Chastity can begin to cause difficulties never envisaged. The Lord seems so remote, so silent and, often, so unreal. The earlier intimacy we experienced with him seems to have gone, and, if we are honest, we cannot say that his will is our daily food.

For a number of people these normal experiences are magnified and brought to a crisis point on occasions of serious loss or misunderstanding, or a grave illness, or the death of a friend or parent. A certain sense of dissatisfaction, of discouragement, or perhaps even of disillusionment can begin to pervade one's whole being. We feel that all our efforts are unimportant, if not useless. Difficulties, obstacles, and even persecution begin to multiply, coming at times from where we least expected them, even from those with whom we work or from superiors or bishops.

We become tired; we yearn for independence, to do something more interesting, to be in charge of our own lives. Or there can be a desire to "settle down," to do only what is indispensable, without searching, without changing, without creativity. The great temptation of this crisis is to compromise. We look for some comfortable position somewhere between the Gospel and the "world", so that while we display a sincere exterior, something that appears "intact," we have closed in upon ourselves, losing all the dynamism of discipleship and love.

These difficulties place before us crucial alternatives: either to remain in a discouraged and mediocre state or to choose again the radicalism of the Gospel more maturely. For most of us, the greatest temptation is to drop anchor in the calm waters of mediocrity. If these experiences are to lead me to growth, to a new direction in my life, it is of crucial importance that I have to resist the temptation to deny them by repressing them, or by running away from them to excessive work, or alcohol, or drugs, or TV, or novel reading, or to any of the other myriad ways of escaping.

I have to be ready to enter into and accept the mystery of my own existence. The genuine love and self-giving to which Jesus has called each one of us and on which I want to focus, is only possible in the measure that I allow these experiences to lead me to understand myself at ever deeper levels. I must face, accept and love the self I am discovering; say "yes" to who I am, with my limitations, my selfishness, my fears, possessiveness as well as to my positive qualities and gifts, knowing that there is nothing that I have that I have not received through the creative love of God for me. This kind of acceptance is an act of faith in the God who created me in love and who continually calls me into being to become my truest self. Do I really believe that God loves me as I am now and not as I would like to be?

It is in the finding and accepting of this self that I am further challenged to die to those aspects of my being that I see lead me to focus on my self, on my own satisfaction, ambitions, cravings. At the heart of this challenge is a call to turn away from myself and focus my eyes "only on Jesus". It means living with great ambitions and enthusiasms, but for the building of Jesus' Kingdom, not my own.

I am being called to see with a clearer view of things, to begin my life again with a new perspective on what it means to live poorly, chastely, obediently, lovingly, compassionately, prayerfully. This means experiencing a new kind of presence to God, myself and others. This implies a humility and a healthy mistrust of myself, a readiness to search for the truth, to be led like a disciple even "where I don't want to go", to be guided by the word of God, to walk in its strength; above all it means to recognize that, humanly speaking, it is impossible to live this life fully in a creative life-giving way, but that, with the power of God's Spirit, all things are possible.

Each of us is being called and each of us remains free before the Lord — free to say "yes" or "no" to him — at this decisive stage in our following of him, when we are being invited to a much deeper level of commitment. When God calls me then at this stage of my life, he wants to break through that self-centeredness that is so deeply rooted in all of us. To surrender myself to this transforming work of God demands a discipline — not a discipline of rigorous control, but one of actively allowing myself to be led by the Spirit. Only God's love is capable of taking me out of myself, even sometimes against my own natural desires, in order to give myself in service to others.

Once during a recollection day I asked a group of priests to share something of their own spirituality with each other. One of the priest gave this account of his spiritual journey. "When I was a young priest, I felt I had to do something for the Lord. I had to love him and my neighbor. I had to make sure that the Kingdom would not remain just an ideal, but would really come alive in my parish. I worked hard in those years with much zeal and determination. It was a good time. In all modesty I can say that I was quite successful. But lately as I get older I hear a voice in me which says: 'Well Bill, what you do with all your zeal and effort for the Kingdom is fine. But why don't you now start letting me love you first?' The more I listened to that voice, the more peaceful, the more free and joyful I became. Sure, I still do all the things I did before, but now I do them with an inner conviction and experience that he loves me. And what a difference it makes!"

As with the apostles, that initial call was to leave the things we possessed — a trade, profession, home, the possibility of a family of our own, land, a multiplicity of material things. But on the Lake of Galilee after the Resurrection when the apostles looked as though they were once more becoming absorbed in these things, Jesus called them away again, as is expressed in his dialogue with Peter, not just from things and activities, but from their very selves.

John says in this passage that Jesus was indicating the kind of death Peter was to die. And what was that death if not the daily dying to his own egoism, his own impetuosity, his own fears? And yet it is comforting to note that, despite his ever deepening love and commitment to Jesus, that even at the end of his life his fears could at times get the better of him. "Quo vadis" tells of Peter leaving Rome at the height of Nero's persecution. On the way out of the city he is surprised to encounter Jesus. When Peter asked him where he was going, Jesus replied, "To Rome, to be crucified again." Peter, humbled yet strengthened by this meeting, returned to Rome and was able to finally surrender his life for Jesus and his Kingdom.

Perhaps God's plan for my or your life will not be quite as dramatic as it was for Peter, but for each of us it is not the "what" of our lives that gives them their value. It is, rather, a question of how clearly they reveal God's unconditional love for each of us.

Any mature disciple will by necessity follow the road of Peter. Each one of us will have to undergo a similar "CONVERSION" different from our first commitment to the Lord. For many this might be the most difficult crisis they will have to face in their vocation. The Lord is asking them to allow him to "lead them where they rather would not go."

> "To leave everything" does not lie in leaving one's boat and one's nets and in following Jesus faithfully for a certain time, but going as far as Calvary, receiving the lessons and the fruit of it, and with the help of the Holy Spirit, carrying through with a life which shall find its complete fulfillment in "going where one would rather not like to go." (R. Voillaume, Founder of the Little Brothers of Jesus)

St Ignatius distinguishes three classes of Christians according to the question of their readiness to follow the Lord. To which of the three classes do you belong?

First, Ignatius says, there are those people who say they would like to give their whole life to God, to surrender to him, but they make no use of the means available. They are indecisive and without discipline in their lives, and, therefore, they are not really disciples. Their favorite phrase is, "I would like to...I wish...(Mk 10:17-31). They could be called the WISH-BONE TYPES (will-less).

Second, there are those people who want to tell God what they will do for him. They might simply be energetic or they might be full of generosity, even full of zeal for the Kingdom, but there are still areas of their hearts that need conversion. It is as though they are saying to God, "I'll tell you what I will do for your, Lord." Oftentimes this means anything but what God is really asking. The decisions are to be made on their terms. We could call these people the JAW-BONE TYPES (willful).

Finally, there are those who come before the Lord saying, "Tell me what you wish me to do, your servant is listening. Meanwhile, I will beg and plead for your strength to cope with whatever makes me fearful, or seems beyond me." This person could be characterized as the BACK-BONE TYPES (authentic willing).

QUESTIONS FOR REFLECTION

1. Have I undergone such a conversion as Peter did? Where am I now on the road to mature discipleship?

2.Listen to Jesus questioning you as he did Peter: "Do you love me more than anything and anyone?"

3.What is the real motivating force of my life? On what are my eyes actually set...on my self? success? accomplishment? others? another?

4.Do I really believe that God loves me as I am now? Am I ready to surrender to that love? (Jn 21:18-19).

Story for Reflection:

THE GOLDEN GRAIN OF RICE

I walked from door to door
along the village road, a beggar looking for alms.
In the distance I could see your golden coach
glistening as in a dream.
I asked myself
who this king of kings might be.
My hopes surged, and it seemed that all my dreary days had vanished.
I stood, awaiting alms — given without asking;
riches scattered in the dust.

The coach stopped right next to me.
Your glance fell upon me.
You descended from your coach with a smile.
I sensed that finally I was to be granted true happiness.

Then suddenly you opened your hand and said,
"What do you have to give me?"

Oh, what irony I thought — to beg from a beggar.
I was confused and stood dismayed, not knowing what to do.
Out of my bag I slowly pulled the smallest grain of rice
and handed it to you.

Yet how great was my surprise,
when at the end of the day I emptied out my bag
and found among the grains that fell

a tiny grain of gold
among a lot of worthless things.

Tears welled up and with all my heart I wished
that I had possessed the courage
to have given you **ALL THAT I POSSESSED - MYSELF**.

(R. Tagore in P. Jacobi, *Damit Unser Leben gelingen kann*)

PAUL'S JOURNEY TO MATURE DISCIPLESHIP

Introduction

I have presented to you the journey St. Peter had to take until he was on the right path to become a true disciple of Jesus; until he was willing to "drop behind his Master" and to be led by him the way without hesitation and resistance. The Bible places his journey between the two miraculous catches of fish: Luke 5 which marks his first conversion and John 21 which leads to his second one.

It was a very painful journey but in the end Peter knew where to place his trust: on the love of the Lord for him and his love for the Lord. Nothing else could ever assure him of becoming a true disciple of his Lord. He had not only to leave behind him boat, family and country but also himself, and to rely only on the love of the Master for him and nothing else. On this love of Jesus for him Peter can base his future and the ministry the Lord entrusted to him.

Now we will look at the other great apostle, Paul and see whether he underwent a similar conversion before he discovered how to follow the Lord on the right path; until he could say:

"FOR ME TO LIVE MEANS CHRIST!"

1. Paul's first conversion

Like Peter, Paul must have heard about Jesus long before his conversion took place. As a prominent Pharisee he must have run into Jesus somewhere. Jesus' way of interpreting the Law and offering salvation to everyone, especially to sinners and outcasts, must have upset him very much. These were unthinkable methods for a true Pharisee. The fact that after the death of Jesus a sect of his followers spread his message all over Judea and Samaria drove him to action. He must have thought this message extremely dangerous, otherwise his violent behavior would not be understandable.

Paul had made his first recorded encounter with the Lord on the way to Damascus. Acts refers to this encounter three times in detail: Ac 9:1-19; 22:6-16; 26:12-18. Paul describes it himself in Ga 1:15-16 and refers to it fairly explicitly seven times.

If someone would have asked Paul, just before his death, what he, Paul, regarded as the most decisive moment of his life, he undoubtedly would have replied: the vision on the road to Damascus. This encounter remained for Paul for ever the "Galilee of his life," the spring of his vocation. To this experience he later returned frequently for courage, affirmation, strength and new light. There he saw his entire life in a whole new way and experienced the transforming power of the risen Lord.

It was the Risen Lord that fascinated him all his life. On this "having seen the Risen Lord" he based his right to be acknowledged as an apostle like the rest of those who had seen the Risen Christ.

His whole world has undergone a revolutionary change; what he formerly thought important now seems negligible to him and holds no importance at all. The things which he would never have renounced before, he now considers as so much rubbish because the knowledge of Christ has assumed absolute primacy for him and fills every aspect of his life. The encounter, knowledge and fullness of Christ have completely altered his previous judgments and values. The Damascus event is much more complex than a simple case of moral conversion or change of mind. It is something so profound that we should approach it with great humility and reverence, realizing that we know and understand very little about it (Carlo Martini, *Testimony*).

But if we look a little closer we will realize that it took Paul a long time before his attitudes and behavior were able to catch up with his new insights. Chapter 7 of his letter to the Romans gives us a vivid presentation of this struggle.

2. Paul's vocation crisis

After Paul's dramatic conversion and after his sight had been restored by Ananias - for sure a humiliating experience for him - he immediately started preaching Christ with as much fire and zeal as he had previously railed against him and his followers. After all, he was the theologian and as such he knew best how Christ had to be seen and interpreted in the setting of the Old Testament.

Consequently, after three years he had so antagonized the Jews that he had to be rescued and was taken to Jerusalem by Barnabas. There he was accepted but not exactly welcomed with open arms or with much enthusiasm. There, too, his fearless preaching seemingly made everyone feel uneasy, to say the least. They sent him back to Tarsus from where he came, meaning in effect, they sent him into exile. The Acts of the Apostles cryptically say, "Now the churches throughout Judea, Galilee and Samaria were left in peace." (Ac 9:31)

The exile actually lasted seven years, something worth recalling. Paul was then in his thirties, the prime of his life. He had sacrificed his whole career. He was the only highly trained theologian among all of the apostles. He had a first class education, a vast knowledge of Scripture and the whole Jewish tradition. He was in a position to argue with any learned scholar among the Jews. The rest of the apostles and disciples were just uneducated fishermen in dire need of a man like him in their daily encounter with their learned opponents. But instead of hailing him as God-sent, they forced him into exile. He was not only unneeded, they did not even want him.

The question he might have pondered a hundred times over was: why did the Lord divest me of all that was most precious to me if I am to remain an outsider to the "followers of the way?" How much loneliness did he experience, how often must he have questioned the initial moment of his encounter and the vision he had? How did he cope with all that? Paul never elaborated on this matter.

The ten years after his first conversion were years of difficulty, of clashes and uneasiness caused by his over-fiery preaching methods and his taking too many risks. They were also years of loneliness, silence and discouragement. Paul had the skills, he had the tools. But something was still lacking.

Once upon a time there was a young man
And this young man dearly loved to be a blacksmith
So he learned all the necessary techniques of the trade
How to hold the tongs
How to lift the sledge
How to smite the anvil
Even how to blow the glowing fire with the bellows

Having finished his apprenticeship
He was chosen to be employed at the smithy of the Royal Palace
However, his new found delight soon came to an end
When he discovered that he had failed to learn how to kindle a spark
All the skills and knowledge in handling the tools were of no avail
For he had failed to learn how to kindle the spark.

(Paul J. Wharton)

In my life I encountered a few people who had undergone a similar conversion like Paul. Everything appeared to them in a new light and yet the real challenge for them was how to integrate their life into this marvelous vision. Having seen the Lord did not change their character, did not take away their inconsistencies and ingrained sinful habits. It took them often years before that instant conversion gradually was penetrating their whole life and started to really change their behavior and attitudes. Paul's case follows the same pattern.

What happened to Paul was what frequently happens in the case of a total and rapid conversion when everything appears in the best and most favorable light and the motive behind the conversion is not a change of camps or allegiance but the vision of a new life offered in Jesus: something completely new happens, which is the work of God. But when one tries to take up one's daily life, one is left with the same personality. And Paul throws himself into his new mission with the same enthusiasm with which he had attacked the old one; he transfers his zeal from one camp to another and goes back to embracing the work as if it belonged to him. At this point the Lord permits a time of very hard and testing purification so that he may learn that conversion has not merely made him change his field of activity but has given him a new way of life, a new way of looking at things, and he must, as it were, steep himself in this new outlook before it becomes part of his personality. His ideas and words were clear enough; but his instinctive behavior was still the same as it had been before. Through painful experience, Paul comes to realize the very simple truth that God is Lord and that God's minister must prepare himself by emptying his heart of all personal achievements so that he may become more and more a versatile instrument in the hands of God. (Carlo Martini, *Testimony*)

3. Paul's second conversion

If we read his letters correctly it seems that at the end of all this he had a second powerful encounter with the Lord as recorded in 2 Co 12. This seems to have become for him what the Tiberias experience was to Peter. He refers to a vision he had fourteen years previously. In these years of solitude and loneliness he came to **KNOW** God in a different way. It was the time when the Lord took him under his tutorship, when he had to **BE WITH THE LORD** as the other disciples had been with him before.

A profound purification took place. He came to see how much importance he had placed on his upbringing, education, achievements and how these things had held center-stage in his life, although perhaps not consciously.

He came to realize that nothing in this new way of life mattered except that Christ would take over. Paul was gradually moved out of center-stage and Christ gradually became his all in all. He learned not to allow himself to rely on himself and his abilities but on Christ and his love for him.

In this light that we should look at what he says in Ph 3:4-14:

> What I had regarded as an advantage I now come to realize as having been a great disadvantage. All the things that I once thought very worthwhile — now I've thrown them all away so that I can put my trust and hope in Christ alone. Now I have given up everything else — I have found it to be the only way to really know Christ and to experience the mighty power that brought him back to life again, and to find out what it means to suffer and to die with him.

Paul, like Peter, had finally come to accept his own weaknesses and to put all his trust into Christ's love for him.

> "Paul begins to be a pastor after Christ's heart after fifteen years of labor and suffering. He does not do this by his own efforts but by the gift of God. The fundamental means of achieving transfiguration is to realize that it is God, in his mercy, who brings it about" (C. Martini, *Testimony*).

In 1982 Pope John Paul II canonized Fr. Maximilian Kolbe, a Polish Franciscan, who gave his life so that the father of a family might be saved from the gas chamber. At the time of his beatification some years later a television interviewer asked this man whose life had been spared what it felt like to have been saved from death, to have another man die that one might himself be spared. The saved man replied, "Ever since that day I feel that I have been walking in another man's shoes. I feel impelled to live with his attitudes, by the values for which he lived and died."

4. PAUL AFTER HIS SECOND CONVERSION

Seemingly Paul was not a very striking or attractive person nor a gifted orator. (Someone once fell asleep during his sermon and Paul had to bring him back to life.) But his fervor, his whole-hearted commitment to Christ made him so powerful in his words and presence that none of his opponents could remain unimpressed (2 Co 12).

He finally had become a true disciple of Jesus. **"Life for me means Christ."** And there is only one desire left for him: "All I want is to know Christ and to experience the power of his resurrection so that I may be able to go with him down to Jerusalem."

There is a very important statement in this text which we should not overlook. For Paul to be a disciple is never something accomplished, it is always a 'becoming a disciple,' it is a journey towards becoming one, it is a process that might take a whole life time with many trials and errors. Paul is absolutely convinced of the power of the Risen Lord operative in him. He knows that this power will lead him to the end of the long journey where he will see Christ face to face.

He knows very well that he has not yet reached this goal and, therefore, twice he makes it very clear to his readers lest they believe otherwise.

Brethren, I really do not think that I have reached it already...I do not claim that I have already succeeded in this, all I do is to stretch myself out towards it...

What a consolation for you and me. Who of us would claim that he or she has reached perfect discipleship yet? All we can do is to start again and again, constantly reaching out and starting anew with the firm knowledge that the Lord is there with his love and his power to lead us on. He will always be there going before us; all we are asked to do is to fall behind him like his first disciples.

Texts in the epistle that refer explicitly to the Damascus event

Ga 1:15-16- the only basic text of the vision
Rm 8:29-30- refers to his own experience in a general setting
1 Co 9:1- he 'saw' the Lord
1 Co 15:8-9 - "he appeared to me, too.."
Ph 3:4-9- Paul, before and after the event

2 Co 4:6 - from darkness to light

1 Tm 1:12-13 - "I who was first a blasphemer"

Questions for Reflection:

1.Has my experience been in any way similar to that of Paul? How?

2.What are the possessions which prevent me from making a free response to God's initiative in my life?

3.Who is the object of my zeal? What is the quality of my zeal? Have I had any particularly difficult experience which has made me change my attitudes?

Story for Reflection:

THE TOUCH OF A MASTER'S HAND

"It was battered and scarred, and the auctioneer
Thought it scarcely worth his while
To waste much time on the old violin
But held it up with a smile
"What am I bidding, good folks," he cried,
"Who'll start the bidding for me?"
"A dollar, a dollar"; then, "Two!" only two?
Two dollars, and who'll make it three?
"Three dollars, once; thee dollars, twice;
Going for three -" But no,
From the room, far back, a gray haired man
Came forward and picked up the bow;
Then wiping the dust from the old violin,
And tightening the loose string,
He played a melody pure and sweet
As a caroling angel sings.

The music ceased, and the auctioneer,
With a voice that was quiet and low,
Said, "What am I to bid for the old violin?"
And he held it up with the bow.
"A thousand dollars, and who'll make it two?
Two thousand! And who'll make it three?

Three thousand once, three thousand twice
And going, and gone," said he.

The people cheered, but some of them cried:
"We do not quite understand
What changed its worth."
Swift came the reply:
"The touch of a master's hand."

(Myra Brooks Welch)

AFFIRMING HIS PRESENCE: PRAYER OF REMINISCENCE

Introduction

Prayer of reminiscence is a prayer that aims at helping us to become aware of two things. First, of God's presence in our lives as a God who loves us unconditionally; second, of the need to come to grips with the hurt we have experienced but have not yet fully integrated into our lives.

Before we start this prayer, one requirement is absolutely necessary — that we first put ourselves consciously into the presence of God and become aware that he is there listening attentively to us and wanting to heal us where we need healing most.

Remember All the Good Things God Has Done For You and Has Given You

If we search our lives we can and will find numerous occasions on which God has shown us in many different ways his love and concern. We should always keep in mind what Gandhi once said, "God always reveals himself to us in some concrete shape." To discover him in my life I have to seek out these "concrete shapes" through which he revealed himself to me.

I can start from the present and move backward as far as I can in remembering my earliest days of childhood, or I can begin with my childhood and move forward to the present time. In relation to this, there are four main areas we will consider:

a) PERSONS: God does not deal with us directly, but most of the time he reveals himself through other persons such as our mother, our father, or people who have really shaped our lives. They have done much for us and their influence in our lives has affected what we are now.

As a seminarian I did some pastoral work with prison inmates who were 16 to 18 years old. They all told me the story of their lives and why they had ended up where they then were. This had two effects on me. First, I realized that it was not virtue on my part that I had not ended up like they, but most probably, it was only because I had lacked opportunities to go wrong. If I had been born into their life-situation and surroundings, how could I be sure that I would have behaved differently from their way of acting? Second, it really made me thankful and grateful to all the people who had raised me, shaped me, and who gave me a true example of a Christian life.

b) JOYS: We should often recall the small joys in our lives we have experienced so frequently and have perhaps taken for granted. If I am convinced of God's love for me, I will discover his love for me behind even the smallest things. As Bernanos says, "There is not the smallest incident in our lives behind which we cannot discover his providence."

c) SPECIAL MOMENTS OF GRACE: In each person's life there are moments of intense experience, when one feels particularly graced. Every person will have at least a few 'peak experiences' when he or she will feel God's presence almost physically. It could be a moment when we have been protected from great danger or have had an intense experience of God's loving presence.

One incident that happened during my childhood convinced me that God had a particular interest in me. After the war, there was much abandoned ammunition left scattered in the fields around my home village. One day I found a hand-grenade. Not knowing what it was I looked for some tools to get at the core of the matter! Strangely enough, no tool could be found. My mother, who generally never bothered much about what we village children were playing suddenly became interested in why I so urgently wanted a hammer. Going back with me to the group of expectant playmates, she discovered to her horror what I had wanted to do with the hammer, had I found one.

I am sure everyone has similar experiences. The question is how we look at them.

d) IMPORTANT DAYS IN OUR LIFE: Graduation day, or entrance into religious life, or first or final profession, ordination, a birthday, a jubilee. These are days on which one can be more aware of God's choice, of his guidance and goodness.

Prayer of remembrance can easily be supported by Scripture texts, such as Psalms 103 or 145.

Bless Yahweh, my soul, bless his holy name, all that is in me! Bless Yahweh, my soul, and remember all his kindness: in forgiving all your offenses, in curing all your diseases, in redeeming your life from the Pit, in crowning you with love and tenderness, in filling your years with prosperity, in renewing your youth like an eagle's (Ps 103:1-5).

I sing your praises, God my King, I bless your name for ever and ever, blessing you day after day, and praising your name for ever and ever (Ps 145:1).

The Magnificat or other canticles of Scripture could be used as well. They should lead us into a prayer of "day-dreaming", marveling about all God has done for us. On special days we should spend some time in such prayer and end the day with a joyful, thankful attitude, knowing more deeply how good and kind the Lord has been to us through each and every day of our lives.

Remember the Past: The Times Others Have Hurt You

We all receive hurts in our lives. To forgive is a gift. Often it is not something we can accomplish naturally. We are more likely to want an eye for an eye, and often two eyes for one. Frequently our attitude is, "I will forgive you but I will not forget." That doesn't suffice. If we want to remain or become wholesome and mature persons, we need to forgive and to overcome the hurt in our lives. To do this we need to be healed.

There are different ways to accomplish this. Which way is the best for us depends on how deeply we have been hurt and how severe the wounds still are at present. Here are some ways of dealing with memories of hurt:

1. A good way to start is to get the hurt out of us by talking about it, bringing it into the open, not letting it remain down in the recesses of our heart where it can become like a cancer. Once it is in the open, it is not so threatening. We can assess it more objectively and strip it of all the further hurts that have accumulated over it with the years.

2. Bring it before the Lord for healing. In his presence the hurt can come alive again with all the bitter feelings, anger and thoughts of revenge you had when it first happened. Place them in front of him. Jesus came to heal people like you and me, angry and embittered people.

Often it is the realization of what God has done and is doing for me day after day that can give me the strength to forgive. The Parable of the Unforgiving Servant could serve as a beautiful text for reflection. "Could you not forgive your brother that little amount after I had forgiven you so much" (Mt 18: 21-35).

I like to tell people that it might be a good practice to insert into their prayer-life the "prayer of complaint". This means that once in a while they should go before the Lord and present to him all they want to complain about. The effect can be healing and refreshing.

One of the most devastating things that can happen to a priest or a religious is that he or she becomes an embittered and angry person the older he or she gets. It is an astonishing and sad fact that this happens more often than we think. At the root of such bitterness one finds quite often a hurt done many years previously by a person in authority. Perhaps one was ordered to take an assignment one did not want, or refused one that one did want. Perhaps a project was not approved, or preference was wrongly given to others. The result: deep hurt. But this hurt was never really dealt with to make sure it was healed. Often it was covered up with a few pious phrases and pushed back into the recesses of the unconscious.

If you feel that way, make every effort and use every means to get rid of it, otherwise it might destroy your life or at least, prevent you from being a happy and a joyful person. It is sad to see a religious person trying to fulfill all his or her religious obligations, such as prayer and apostolic work, and yet, at a close glance, to realize how much bitterness and resentment exist in this person. One wonders how both can exist so closely together.

What should be done in such a case? Pray with all your strength for healing. Not just once but constantly expose your hurt to the Lord and cry to him like the blind Bartimaeus, "Lord Jesus, have mercy on me!"

They came to Jericho. As Jesus was leaving with his disciples and a large crowd, a blind man named Bartimaeus, the son of Timaeus, was sitting by the road, begging. When he heard that it was Jesus of Nazareth, he began to shout, "Jesus! Son of David! have mercy on me!" Many scolded him and told him to be quiet. But he shouted even more loudly, "Son of David, have mercy on me!" Jesus stopped and said, "Call him." So they called the blind man. "Cheer up!" they said. "Get up, he is calling you." He threw off his cloak, jumped up, and came to Jesus. "What do you want me to do for you?" Jesus asked him. "Teacher," the blind man answered, "I want to see again." "Go," Jesus told him, "your faith has made you well." At once he was able to see, and followed Jesus on the road (MK 10:46-52).

3. If the hurt is deeply rooted we might have to look for other people to help us. It could be a spiritual director or, in a more severe case, a psychiatrist might be needed. What is most important is that we do something about it and not let it ruin our lives. It is still difficult for many of us to accept the fact that there are situations in our lives where we cannot help ourselves anymore and do need professional help. God can and does demand that kind of humility from us that will lead us to go to someone and tell him or her, "I cannot handle this by myself anymore, I need your help."

I once had to deal with a hurt in my life and I prayed hard to God for healing. One day someone told me about a person who evidently had a true gift of healing people like myself. But because of my pride, I felt reluctant to go there and ask for her assistance. After all, I was a theologian, and she was "just" a house wife. And so I queried God, "Why can't you heal me directly? Why do I have to go through all this?" The hurt and pain continued until I finally went and asked this person for help. It was only then that I felt healing take place. I had suffered more than was necessary through my own fault, but in the end, I came to the realization that God reaches us through the gifts of other persons. We cannot handle everything ourselves.

Remember the Times You Have Hurt Others

We not only receive hurts ourselves but we hurt other people as well and in the same way as we have been hurt. We have to remember that there might be people who are suffering now from bitterness or resentment which we have caused in them. Even though we might have hurt them unintentionally. It is also quite likely that many of those whom we have hurt purposely are out of our reach. We cannot go to them anymore and ask for forgiveness.

There is, however, a way to reach them and to help them. We can ask Christ to heal the wounds we have inflicted on them. He can touch them and reach them where they most need his help. We should remember these people and also, if still possible, bring before our minds very concretely the hurt we have done them and then ask the Lord to liberate them from resentment, anger and bitterness.

Our Relationship to God

There are two other related questions which I have to face: "How do I look at myself?" and, "Am I angry with God?"

1.DO I ACCEPT MYSELF AS I AM?

As I came from God? Do I accept my physical shape, character traits, the talents I have, the way I was brought up?

There are many scriptural texts that can help us here, texts for the proud as well as for the ones whose self-image is rather low. The proud could meditate on what Paul has to say about how God kept him from being proud because of the knowledge he had received in visions (2 Co 12:7-13):

His answer was, "My grace is all you need; for my power is strongest when you are weak." I am most happy, then to be proud of my weaknesses, in order to feel the protection of Christ's power over me. I am content with weaknesses, insults, hardship, persecutions, and difficulties for Christ's sake. For when I am weak, then I am strong."

For those of us who suffer from low self-esteem, Psalm 139 gives us a beautiful picture of how we should look at ourselves.

For it was you who created my being, knit me together in my mother's womb. I thank you for the wonder of my being, for the wonders of all your creation.

This psalm is so simple in its content it does not need interpreting to be understood. What is important is that we make sure we have the right image of God. We must read this psalm in the light of a God whom Jesus revealed to us as unconditional love, a God who knows every detail of our lives, all our thoughts, because he loves us. He was there when each one was "knit together". Each person is his handiwork.

God had a dream when he thought of you, a dream of something beautiful. You are meant to express something of his being that no one else could or will ever express. God made a billion snapshots of himself and you are one of them. St. Paul expresses this thought in his own way, marvelling at God's incomprehensible love which he showed us in the death of his Son for us when we were still sinners. We have to look at ourselves and all of creation from the perspective of that love.

It has been said that my spiritual identity depends on how far I discover this "uniqueness", the dream God had in creating me. Someone once commented, "Yes, God had a beautiful dream when he thought of you and created you, but many of his beautiful dreams have turned into nightmares for him.

But since Jesus came and has revealed to us the true nature of God and how we are to understand his all-pervasive presence in our lives there can only be amazement, wonder and awe: we never knew that God could be like that. In whatever situation we find ourselves God is there, offering us a new future full of hope. Every situation, however bad it may be, can be "paschalized", i.e., can lead to a new birth, to a resurrection. What seems to be a "stumbling block" to you and me is for God a "stepping stone" for you and me. The question is, will we use it as such?

From the Middle Ages comes this legend about a nun who claimed that she had a vision of Christ. The bishop asked, "Sister, did you talk to him?" And she said, "Yes, I did." He continued, "If you have another vision, ask Christ this question: 'What was the bishop's greatest sin before he became a bishop?'" He knew that only God and his own confessor would know. About three months later, the nun made an appointment to see the bishop. When she came in, he said, "Did you see our Lord again?" "Yes," she replied. "Did you ask him the question about my sin?" "Yes, I did." "And what did he say?" She smiled and answered, "The Lord said, 'I don't remember anymore.'" (Paul J. Wharton)

What can ever separate us from the love of God in Jesus Christ?

God's care and love for you is also expressed in these texts:

I made you...in my own image and likeness, and when I made you I saw that you are good (Gn 1:27;31).

You are my work of art (Ep 2:10).

You...are part of my household (Ep 2:22).

You...reflect like a mirror the brightness of the Lord and grow brighter as you turn into the image that you reflect. This is my work (2 Co 3:10).

A mature person is one who enjoys what he or she is, who is always open to growth, who can GIVE by being creative and productive for others and who can receive and take in what is offered by others.

And so I am led to ask the question: Am I able to thank God for the wonder that I am?

2. Am I Angry With God?

There are people who are angry with God. Something happened in their life with which they were never able to cope. Very often, it's the death of a beloved person like a mother or father. Or it may have been some personal defeat. They blame God for it and are not able to work through this problem.

This can block the way to a happy and mature spiritual life. It can keep us enclosed in ourselves and doomed to remain spiritually immature for the rest of our lives. The prayer of reminiscence is a prayer that should stir us to growth in spirituality. It helps us to realize the loving presence of God in our lives and to remove the blocks that might be in the way of a deep and lasting relationship with Him.

Story for Reflection:

THE LOOK OF JESUS

In Luke's Gospel we read:
"Peter said, 'Man I do not know what you are talking about.' At that moment, while he was still speaking, a cock crew; and the Lord turned and looked straight at Peter... and Peter went outside and wept bitterly."

I had a fairly good relationship with the Lord. I would ask him for things, converse with him, praise him, thank him...

But always I had this uncomfortable feeling that he wanted me to look into his eyes. And I would not. I would talk, but look away when I sensed he was looking at me.

I always looked away. And I knew why. I was afraid. I thought I should find an accusation there of some unrepented sin. I thought I should find a demand there - there would be something he wanted from me.

One day, I finally summoned up courage and looked! There was no accusation. There was no demand. The eyes just said, "I love you." I looked searchingly. Still, the only message was, "I love you!"

And I walked out and, like Peter, I wept.

(A. Mello, *The Song of the Bird*)

FOLLOWING THE CONTEMPLATIVE LORD: PRAYER AND DISCIPLESHIP

Introduction

In explaining in more detail what it means to follow the Lord, which is the essential and most important vocation of our life, I would like to talk now about prayer as part of this call to discipleship.

There are hundreds of books on prayer, and every day new books appear on the market. The majority of these books deal with such topics as how to learn to pray again, better prayer, methods of prayer, why we should pray, the effect of prayer. In short, all aspects of prayer seem to be covered fairly well. Why, then, should I take up this topic once again, since I can't say anything new?

As with all topics in theology and spirituality, once they become popular, it is all the more necessary to go back to their roots. In this case, this means going back to Jesus himself. Since being a disciple of Christ means to follow his life style and to carry on his mission, the simple question is this: What importance did Jesus give to prayer in his life and what did he expect, in the area of prayer, from those who would follow him?

There are two dimensions of Christ's mission: a downward and an upward movement.

DOWNWARD MOVEMENT: Jesus brings us God's unconditional love, wanting to establish with us that intimate relationship in which our salvation consists. He is God's offer of salvation to us.

UPWARD MOVEMENT: Jesus, identifying himself with us, being one with us, also responds to the offer of God's love for us, and in so doing, he makes it a reality for us. He is our representative who, by giving an answer for us, makes the covenant with God come true once and for all.

In prayer Jesus gave the response to God's offer of love. Prayer for him meant drawing the whole human race, with whom he had identified himself, into God's own lifestream. The Church has taken up this mission of Christ. She too has to care for these two dimensions: the APOSTOLIC dimension, which is to preach and offer again and again God's in-breaking Kingdom to all; and the RELIGIOUS dimension, which is her response to what she herself has received, in thanksgiving, adoration and praise, so that she is drawn into the lifestream of the Triune God. But she does this not only for her own sake but also as the representative of all human beings and of creation as a whole. This response she gives officially in the liturgy.

Did Jesus Pray?

If Jesus was a fully human person (Ph 2:6-11), then we may say, "Of course he did." Jesus grew up in a devout Jewish home. That means he prayed three times a day with his parents: in the morning, at noon, and in the evening. Besides saying these daily prayers, he participated in the liturgical heritage of his people. He went to the synagogue on the Sabbath "as was his custom" (Lk 4:16). J. Jeremias, who studied the prayer life of Jesus extensively, summarizes his examination,

> So we may conclude with all probability that no day in the life of Jesus passed without his observing the three times of prayer: morning prayer at sunrise, afternoon prayer at the time when the afternoon sacrifice was offered in the temple, evening prayer at night before going to sleep. We can sense from this something of the hidden inner life of Jesus, something of the source from which he daily drew his strength. (J. Jeremias, *Prayers of Jesus*)

Jesus, however, seemed not to be content with the practice of liturgical prayer three times a day. Of particular interest here are the references to prayer in solitude. There are six passages in the Gospel which describe Jesus as praying all night or before sunrise. He either prolongs the evening prayer far into the night or extends his morning prayer by starting long before sunrise.

> Mk 1:35: And in the morning, rising up a great while before day, he went out and departed into a solitary place to pray.

Peter becomes worried and looks for him. Somehow he must have had an inkling where he could find him. Jesus' behavior is important. He does not go back to the crowds, although all are waiting for him, and his success with them seems to be assured. Jesus, having discerned in prayer the will of the Father, feels he has to move on. Prayer is for him the way to get to know the Father's will.

Mk 6:46: And when he had sent them away he departed into a mountain to pray.

The text says later that it was only in the early morning hours that the disciples saw him again. Jesus must have prayed the whole night.

Lk 6:12: He went up to a mountain to pray, and continued all night in prayer to God.

This was the night before he selected the twelve apostles, a task he must have taken very seriously. There are other passage which tell us that Jesus prayed for his disciples. He prayed that Peter would not lose his faith in him during the passion, "I have prayed for you, Simon, that your faith will not fail" (Lk 22:32). In the Gospel of John, Jesus prays for his disciples (17:9), and for all those who will believe in him (17:20). That means Jesus prayed then for you and me as well.

Lk 5:15f: His reputation continued to grow, and large crowds would gather to hear him and have their sickness cured, but he would always go off to some place where he could be alone and pray.

The amazing point here is that the more successful Jesus became, the more he felt the need to pray. Strange to say, we normally behave in the opposite way. Once we are in demand, the danger grows that we may shorten our prayer to make more time for work and people.

Lk 3:21: Now, when all the people had been baptized and while Jesus after his own baptism was at prayer, heaven opened and the Holy Spirit descended on him.

Lk 9:28: Now about eight days after this had been said, he took with him Peter and John and James and went up the mountain to pray. As he prayed, the aspect of his face was changed.

These texts tell us that important things happen to Jesus when he is at prayer. Here he comes to recognize his mission and his true identity. Luke makes the same observation for the early Church in the Acts of the Apostles. Here also the Spirit comes, and decisions are made only when the community or the individual is at prayer. Prayer is the atmosphere in which God discloses himself and the Spirit is sent. Peter was "at prayer" when he had his vision in Jaffa (Ac 11:5).

> Lk 9:18: Now one day when he was praying alone in the presence of his disciples he put this question to them, "Who do people say I am?"

Jesus had no difficulty in praying alone even with all the disciples around him. As Jeremias observes, it was not common to place prayer straight in the middle of daily life. Here it seems as if Jesus, realizing in prayer his intimacy and closeness to the Father, and knowing in prayer who he was, asked his disciples who they thought he was.

> Lk 11:1: Now once he was in a certain place praying and, when he had finished, one of his disciples said, "Lord, teach us to pray."

The praying Jesus must have made a deep impact on the disciples. They saw the strength and joy he drew from prayer, and therefore, they just asked him, "Lord can you give us a share in your prayer?"

In summary, we might say that there should be no argument as to whether Jesus prayed or not. Besides the common liturgical prayer practice, prayer in solitude seems to have been an essential part of Jesus' life, at which he spent a considerable amount of time. That brings us to the second question.

Why Did Jesus Pray?

In Prayer Jesus lived out his being the Son in human form. In prayer he could talk with the Father, since he enjoyed an intimacy such as none of us can ever experience. Prayer came naturally to him, since prayer, according to Teresa of Avila, means, "Being with him whom we know loves us." But this is only one aspect. For it is important to realize that it was in prayer that Jesus found the strength to carry out his mission and to fulfill this mission in the way the Father wanted. He prays as part of his mission. That does not mean Jesus was a contemplative in the sense that he withdrew from the world. He always came back to "the world" after he had spent hours in prayer.

It is a mistake to think that Jesus was always the same, always calm, always in control of himself, a man undisturbed by anything. Jesus was as sensitive to the people and things around him as any other human being, in fact, more so. He was a human being "in everything except sin" (Ph 2:7; Heb 4:15). He had the nerves of a human, the temperament, the patience and the limitations of a human being.

The following passages indicate this more clearly:

He was annoyed with his disciples: Mt 16:8

Men of little faith...Do you not yet understand... how could you fail to understand?

He was irritated: Lk 9:41

Faithless and perverse generation! How much longer must I be among you and put up with you? How unbelieving and wrong you people are!

He was impatient: Mk 8:17-18

Don't you know or understand yet? Are your minds so dull? You have eyes - can't you see? You have ears - can't you hear? Don't you remember?

He cried: Lk 19:41-42

As he drew near and came in sight of the city he shed tears over it and said...

He was overwhelmed by anxiety: Jn 12:27

Now my heart is troubled, and what shall I say? Shall I say, Father, do not let this hour come upon me?

He was discouraged: Mk 14:34

The sorrow in my heart is so great that it almost crushes me.

The Gethsemane prayer (Mt 26:36-46) particularly shows us that Jesus found in prayer the strength to say "yes" to the cross as the Father's will for him. But the Gethsemane struggle was a life-and-death-struggle, as Heb 5:7-8 has it:

In his life on earth Jesus made his prayers and requests with loud cries and tears to God, who could save him from death. Because he was humble and devoted, God heard him. But even though he was God's Son he learned to be obedient by means of suffering.

There were moments in his life when Jesus too was at the end of the rope, exhausted by all those mediocre, covetous people with their petty preoccupations, and without a sense for deeper realities. Seventeen times Jesus asks his disciples, "Are you still without understanding?" In such situations, when he felt blocked and cut off from his own world, "he would always go off to some place where he could be alone and pray" (Lk 5:16).

Jesus had a preference for hilltops and the desert. But he did not go there to stay there. When he returned from prayer, he was himself again. He had once again found the strength to carry on his mission, to give himself again to the people. A good look at the gospels shows that people recognized Jesus better when he prayed than when he worked miracles. Miracles, confirmed the people in their earthly interests, as can be seen in Jn 6:26, when the people are running after Jesus because he could give them all the bread they needed. "You are looking for me because you ate the bread and had all you wanted."

In contrast to this, it is when Jesus talks about the Father whom he experienced constantly in prayer that people come to believe in him. "Many who heard Jesus say these things believed in him" (Jn 8:28-30). His warmth, joy, love and conviction whenever he spoke about his Father must have made such a deep impression on people that they came to believe him when he spoke about the most difficult subject of his mission.

At times, I wonder what it is that will convince people about Christ and his Kingdom — our great works of charity, our impressive buildings, our programs? Or is it ultimately not the convincing way we speak about the Lord and how we experience him in our life and what he means to us?

A great man once said, "The people who have had the greatest and most lasting impact on the Church and society have all been great people of prayer." If this is true, what a man of prayer Jesus must have been. Jesus regarded prayer as part of his mission. He did not redeem the world by his words and deeds alone but also by his prayer.

I would like to conclude with a quotation from a liberation theologian who closes his meditation on Jesus' prayer life with these words:

We know that Jesus, the perfect man and head of humanity, prayed. He prayed, and made prayer one of the focal points of his life. And Jesus, the same yesterday, today and forever, continues his life of prayer together with the Father 'always keenly interceding for us'. This prayer was and is the salvation of humankind, and acts upon and influences what neither technology nor humanity can: sin, liberty, faith, love and redemption. By our prayer we incorporate ourselves into this prayer of Christ and enter in a real way into collaboration with him in the salvation of humanity and of history. God desires our collaboration with him, and in this perspective, prayer, as well as apostolic action, makes us enter fully, beyond human senses and powers, into the mission of Christ. (S. Galilea, *Following Jesus*)

Questions for Reflection:

1. How important is it to me to give priority to regular times of prayer?

2. What is the meaning of prayer in my life?

3. How can I live contemplatively in the midst of a very active apostolate?

Story for Reflection:

THE TEMPLE BELLS

The temple had stood on an island on an island two miles out to sea. And it held a thousand bells. Big bells, small bells, bells fashioned by the best craftsmen in the world. When a wind blew or a storm raged, all the temple bells would peal out in unison, producing a symphony that sent the heart of the hearer into raptures.

But over the centuries the island sank into the sea and, with it, the temple and the bells. An ancient tradition said that the bells continued to peal out, ceaselessly, and could be heard by anyone who listened attentively. Inspired by this tradition, a young man travelled thousands of miles, determined to hear those bells. He sat for days on the shore, opposite the place where the temple had once stood, and listened, listened with all his heart. But all he could hear was the sound of the waves breaking on the shore. He made every effort to push away the sound of the waves so that he could hear the bells. But all to no avail: the sound of the sea seemed to flood the universe.

He kept at his task for many weeks. When he got disheartened he would listen to the words of the village pundits who spoke with unction of the legend of the temple bells and of those who had heard them and proved the legend to be true. And his heart would be aflame as he heard their words...only to become discouraged again when weeks of further effort yielded no results.

Finally he decided to give up the attempt. Perhaps he was not destined to be one of those fortunate ones who heard the bells. Perhaps the legend was not true. He would return home and admit failure. It was his final day, and he went to his favorite spot on the shore to say goodbye to the sea and the sky and the wind and the coconut trees. He lay on the sands, gazing up at the sky, listening to the sound of the sea. He did not resist that sound that day. Instead, he gave himself over to it, and found it was a pleasant, soothing sound, this roar of the waves. Soon he became so lost in the sound that he was barely conscious of himself, so deep was the silence that the sound produced in his heart.

In the depth of that silence, he heard it! The tinkle of a tiny bell followed by another, and another, and another...and soon every one of the thousand temple bells was pealing out in glorious unison, and his heart was transported with wonder and joy.

If you wish to see God, look attentively at creation. Don't reject it; don't reflect on it. Just LOOK at it.

(A. de Mello, *The Song Of The Bird*)

PRAYER AS PART OF OUR MISSION

Introduction

In our last conference we talked about Jesus and prayer and came to the conclusion that Jesus led a very intense prayer life. He regarded prayer not just as the most natural way for him to be with his Father in order to give expression to the intimacy he felt so intensely, but he saw prayer also as part of his mission, as something he had to do as part of his redemptive work for us. This same mission he entrusted to us, "As the Father has sent me, I am sending you" (Jn 20:21). Thus, for us, his disciples, there are therefore, also two aspects from which we have to look at prayer in our call to follow the Lord as disciples: to be with him, and as apostles: to be sent out.

As Disciples: "To be with Him"

Jesus prayed out of a need of his humanity to communicate with the Father and to express his love for him. Only through prayer do we stay in communion with the Lord at all times. Through prayer we are 'with him', we 'abide in him.'

Prayer provides us with the necessary motivation for our apostolate. It gives us the necessary experience of Christ's presence, particularly in difficult situations. Prayer enables us to judge, react and love according to the Gospel. Since our mission consists in communicating an experience, we must deliberately bring to conscious awareness our faith experience that "Christ lives in us." The only way to do this is through prayer.

Prayer, therefore, as a human activity means to make myself present to the Lord within me so that I can make him present and see him present in everybody and everything around me. Without a continuing life of deep prayer there can be, in the long run, no Christian ministry.

As Apostles: "To be sent out"

Jesus redeemed the world not only through his preaching and teaching but also through his prayer life. This aspect is often overlooked. If this is true, then our call to carry on his mission includes this dimension as well. The best example for this aspect of our mission is St. Paul, who never tires of telling his co-workers and his converts to pray at all times. In his letters both aspects of prayer are clearly dealt with. First, there is prayer of praise and thanksgiving as expression of the new life that we have received in Christ Jesus. Second, we find prayer of petition for all human beings and for the spreading of the Gospel. A few texts:

> First of all, then, I urge that petitions, prayer, requests and thanksgiving be offered to God for all (1 Tm 2:1).

> I want all everywhere to pray, all those who are dedicated to God and can lift up their hands in prayer without anger or argument (1 Tm 2:8).

> Pray at all times, be thankful in all circumstances ...Pray also for us, brothers (1 Th 5:17; 25).

For some people prayers of thanksgiving and praise are understandable, but these same people have difficulty with prayers of petition. Can prayer change the course of events? Should we not let things be done by human skill, intelligence and technology? Does prayer have a meaning in a world that is totally explainable and plannable? Is prayer not an evasion of human responsibility?

Prayer as the only way to influence human freedom

We know that God created us free and that he does respect our human freedom to an amazing degree. God cannot and will not impose himself on our freedom. All human efforts and plans are constantly subjected to a reality which we cannot change by our will and power: HUMAN FREEDOM. What determines human history and its outcome is ultimately human freedom.

Only God can influence this freedom without violating it. He alone can influence and change without violation this most precious gift we as human beings have, our freedom on which all personal decision and human history depend. It is in considering HOW God influences individual freedom that we need to take prayer into account. For prayer seems to be able to reach into that realm where human reasoning, human efforts and skills seem at times totally unsuccessful, i.e., the realm of freedom, faith and love.

> Our faith tells us that we have the possibility of influencing the freedom of people in cooperation with God so that they will be willing to convert, to change, to make peace, to reach decisions that can lead to justice, brotherhood and sisterhood without being compelled or forced in any way. This is possible only for God, but he willed that through prayer we can and should participate in his providence and care for all human beings. (S. Galilea, *Following Jesus*)

From this perspective, the saying seems to be correct that the people who have had the most powerful and most lasting influence on the Church and society were all people of great prayer. Prayer must be based on this firm conviction, otherwise we give up praying too easily if we don't see immediate results.

Rabbi Mendel used to say that every single person who asked for his prayer would be present in his mind whenever he would pray the silent prayer of the Eighteen Petitions. Someone who was puzzled by the remark asked, "How is that possible in such short a prayer?" The Rabbi replied, "From the distress of everyone who asked for my prayer, there remains a wound cut into my heart. During the hour of prayer, I open my heart and say, 'Lord of the universe, read what is written down here!' "(Martin Buber, *Erzählungen der Chassidim*)

It was Jesus himself who told us of the all-importance of prayer. The word: "prayer," "praying" or "pray" is found sixty-three times in the four Gospels, most of the time coming from the lips of Jesus himself. We must remember that Christ redeemed the world through his prayer as well as through his deeds and that he continues to pray for us. He has called us to join him in this mission. We become his co-workers even in prayer. Here we enter into the mission of Christ much more deeply than any human power could ever accomplish.

There have been a few incidents in my life that have reenforced that lesson for me. I want to share these experiences with you even though it is true that all personal experiences can be said to be purely subjective.

Some years ago I had the chance to meet a well known clairvoyant. I asked her how it was that so many of her predictions did not come true. In turn, she asked me: "Father, do you believe in prayer?" I said, "Of course, I do." "Well", she said, "then you should know that prayer can change any event of history. If predictions of a negative nature do not come true it could be because some people prayed with fervor and perseverance that they might not happen. I am a religious person, and experience has convinced me of the effectiveness of prayer. Prayer can change the flow of events, and often it is the only means that can bring this about. Prayer has an effect on the hidden recesses of the heart where people make decisions which determine events in history."

If you look at the message delivered by Mary in her apparitions, you can observe the same thing. Mary always connected a condition to the predictions of coming calamities - "if people do not pray." Perhaps many predicted events did not take place for the simple reason that people did indeed pray.

I knew a very competent doctor in the Providence Hospital in Manila who was a good Italian-style Catholic - not much of a church-goer but a religious man in his own way. One day we brought a seriously-ill woman to the hospital. She was a mother of eight children. Dr.S. operated on her, but she was still in a very serious condition. I asked him if there was any hope. He answered me, "Well, Father, all we can do is pray." My response came quickly and was given with evident exasperation. "Is that all you can do, Doctor?" But then it was his turn to be angry. He grabbed me and almost shouted in my face, "You, as a priest, have no faith in prayer! You should be ashamed of yourself. Let me tell you something, Father. I am not much of a Catholic, but this much I know from experience as a physician: if that woman starts fighting back because she found the will to live, I know there is only one explanation - prayer, not medicine has been at work. Prayer alone can influence the will to live and not to give up. If this happens, that for me is a miracle. So you had better start praying..." I remember sneaking away rather shamefaced. But I did start praying in earnest, and the woman did get well again...

Another experience I had, which impressed on me the efficacy of prayer, also happened in the Philippines. I had been asked to give a retreat in a minor seminary. I knew the young rector who had previously been my student. When I finished the retreat he told me with tears in his eyes that he was not able to pay even for my travel expenses. On top of this, he said, the bishop had gone away leaving him with no money, and there was not even enough rice in the kitchen to feed the eighty boys for that day. Shopkeepers had stopped giving him credit because he was so far behind with his payments. Trying to console him, I suggested that we go to the chapel and pray. I don't know what we prayed or how long, but when I came out of the church, a car drove up and a woman stepped out and asked me whether this was the seminary. I said that it was, and asked her if she wanted to speak with the rector. No, that wasn't necessary, she said. Then she went on to explain, "My husband and I were travelling on the highway over there. We are on a holiday trip. Suddenly I remembered that we had made a promise some time ago to show our gratitude for a miraculous recovery of our grandson from a serious illness. I said to my husband, 'Here we are going again on vacation, without having fulfilled our promise.' At that moment, I saw a sign indicating a seminary and I insisted that we call in. Please, take this gift and use it for your needs in this house." She did not even give me time to call the rector. When I found him, the couple had left and we stood there, richer by 1000 Pesos. We prayed once more. There were tears in the eyes of the rector, but this time, they were tears of gratitude.

These instances in my life told me how the prayer of petition works. Who can give a sick person the will to live and with it energize all the life-power in a person? Who can make a person change his or her mind? God has his own way but, it seems he uses ordinary means to work the seemingly miraculous in the life of people.

Some concluding remarks

Prayer is never a waste of time nor does it separate us from our fellow human beings. As in his life, Jesus came to understand his mission better and to grow in love for us through prayer, so it is with us. Prayer will draw us back to people and not away from them. St. Paul demanded from his Christians that they should work hard and pray constantly. He regarded both as an essential part of his own mission. I once asked Mother Teresa of Calcutta what she regarded as the essential characteristics of a good vocation for someone wanting to join her congregation. She said spontaneously, "The capacity and willingness for hard work and a deep faith expressed in a love for prayer." For her, as for Paul, prayer is apostolic work. It means participation in the transformation of the world. In that sense, our whole life can be called a constant prayer.

Yet, one may say, if all actions are prayer why do we need the special activity traditionally called prayer? A response to that question has been rather succinctly expressed in the following quotation: "In practice, you can only pray all of the time everywhere if you bother to pray some of the time somewhere." Without times of prayer, there is a risk that our activity will cease to be impregnated by a prayerful attitude. People do expect from us that we be men and women of prayer. "Father, Sister, pray for me!" are words we often hear. People may not think so highly of you, but when they are in distress, they ask you to pray for them. They regard prayer as our field of expertise and do think that we pray more than they. A priest or a religious who does not pray is dangerous. People expect us to be men and women of faith who habitually look at life and the world in God's way. If they come and ask for our advice, our counsel, they expect an answer that is not based on purely human reasoning, as good as it may be. They expect an answer that comes from a deep life of faith and prayer. What advice can we give if we are not rooted in prayer?

Someone suggested that priests and religious who do not pray should advertise this so that people will be warned. They should wear a T-shirt saying,

"Beware! I am a dangerous priest (or religious) because I don't pray."

In this way people would know what kind of advice they could expect if they approached such a person. We would not be deceiving them.

Christian prayer is meant to be also prayer in the community. This is most beautifully expressed in the Eucharist, which, above all is the prayer of Christ, or better of the whole Christ, head and members, being drawn into the life-circle of the Trinity. It is participation in the life to come, through Christ to the Father in the Holy Spirit. Prayer in community represents the REAL FULLNESS OF CHRISTIAN PRAYER in the sense that Christian prayer, by its very nature, is communal. But the most NECESSARY of all prayer is personal prayer. One might be unable to attend communal prayer but one cannot dispense oneself from personal prayer.

In personal prayer, I exercise my faith. Personal prayer could be called the activity of "naked faith". That is the reason why people with deep faith have always been people of prayer. Faith and prayer are connected in such a way that one demands the other, one goes with the other. In group prayer, I can be carried along. The Eucharist can easily become a substitute for that faith-experience. In personal prayer, such substitution of the external sign for the inner reality is not possible. Personal prayer is a response to our faith-awareness and turns us directly to God. In the long run, we can say that a person who does not pray alone will find it difficult to pray realistically and fully in community. The penalty for not praying is, ultimately, the inability to pray at all!

Since prayer is the most influential means there is to change human hearts and minds, one can understand why many saints had only one ambition, expressed in this statement:

"THERE IS NOTHING I WOULD RATHER BE KNOWN AS THAN
AS A MAN OR A WOMAN OF PRAYER."

Questions for Reflection:

1. Do I pray for "all human beings" and that the Gospel may find an "open door" in their lives, as St Paul asks us to pray?

2. How convinced am I that prayer is one of the most powerful means God has given us to influence the decisions of other people and the flow of history?

3. Can I say that the advice I give to people is based on and accompanied by prayer?

Story for Reflection:

A mother approached the Teacher for assistance with a domestic matter. "My son has horrible eating habits," she said. "Please, he will listen to you if you tell him to stop eating foods with so much sugar."

The Teacher listened sympathetically. "I ask that you come back next week and make the request again."

The mother agreed and returned seven days later. "My son's problem continues," she said. "I am greatly concerned about his health. He rarely eats vegetables or fruits. Please, won't you talk to him about the danger of eating too much sugar."

"Please, come back and see me in a week," the Teacher said simply.

Though the mother was disappointed, she left and returned one week later. Once again she made her plea. This time the Teacher agreed to talk with her son.

When the conversation was completed, the mother thanked the Teacher. "I am grateful that you took the time to talk to my son, but I don't understand why it took three requests for you to do so."

The Teacher looked at the woman and said, "I didn't realize how hard it would be for me to give up sugar."

(W.R. White, *Stories for the Journey*, p.96)

THE RULE OF DISCIPLESHIP: TO FOLLOW THE COMPASSIONATE LORD

Introduction

The norm of conduct Jesus left his disciples and which would forever be the 'Magna Charta' of all their actions, is expressed in these words:

A new commandment I give you; love one another. As I have loved you, so you must love one another. If you have love for one another, then all will know that you are my disciples. (Jn 13:34)

This is my commandment: love one another, just as I have loved you. (Jn 15:12)

The most important words in this commandment seem to be: "AS I." We are not just asked to love but are told that the kind of love we should have, the way we should love is determined by the kind of love Jesus had and by the way he loved us. Christian love must take its measure from Jesus' love, from his "AS I HAVE LOVED YOU." What kind of love is this? The love of Jesus for us is characterized by two basic characteristics: it is UNIVERSAL - and it is COMPASSIONATE love. These two characteristics will always have to remain the points of reference of the question as to how we should love each other and all human beings. The first aspect we will take up later. In this chapter I want to dwell on the second aspect:

Be compassionate as your Father is compassionate. (Lk 6:36)

This almost impossible command remains the ethical foundation of all Christian behavior.

What does it mean to be compassionate?

Generally speaking, many of us believe that we are compassion-ate people, i.e., people who are easily moved by compassion when we see misery and suffering. Is that true? Compassion means literally to "suffer with." We are asked to go where it hurts, to enter the places where people suffer and experience their pain and anguish. We are asked to weep with them, to be vulnerable with them and to be powerless with them. Compassion is, therefore, not just general kindness or tender-heartedness. If understood as "suffering with", it is not a spontaneous human reaction, because all of us protest against such an attitude. We instinctively shun such a demand. We are not meant for suffering. We are pain-avoiders by nature. Compassion is not the central concern of our lives.

> If we look at daily life we will quickly realize that it is not compassion that rules this world but competition. From our childhood on we are told to be different, to compete, to make it, to get ahead, to be first. We are encouraged to conquer life, to create our own identity and to carve out for ourselves a niche from which we can look at the rest of humanity from a distancing vantage-point that makes us unique. From here we can compare ourselves with others and see how we are accepted, known and loved; how we are recognized and famous. We usually mean by compassion that we are kind and gentle to those who have not made it, who have been hurt in the race, but we never want to be the objects of compassion. For many the primary frame of reference in life remains competition, not compassion. (H.Nouwen, D. P. McNeill, D.A. Morrison, *Compassion*)

We have to realize that Jesus' call to his followers to be compassionate goes against our grain, it means a real letting go of ingrained attitudes. Nobody can respond to it except through a total conversion of heart and mind. We have to perceive it as a gift that we receive only in the measure that we let the Kingdom and its power into our lives. Compassion becomes a pattern of behavior only if God's own love takes root in our lives. It is not a purely human virtue, but rather a gift from God.

Our God is a Compassionate God

There are many names given in the Bible to Yahweh, but the most adequate seems to be EMMANUEL, which means GOD IS WITH US. He is a God who belongs to us, who cares for us and who loves to be among us. What does this TO BE WITH really mean?

Who are our real friends? They are those who offer us comfort and consolation in moments of illness, of real suffering, of mental anguish, of distress and loneliness. They are the people who remain with us, who stay with us without saying anything or doing anything. It is this seemingly useless, humble and unpretentious presence in such moments that gives us consolation and comfort. They are the people who would like to say to us, "I don't know what to say or what to do but I want you to realize that I am with you, that I will not leave you." Presence does not mean that I have to be useful. To say, "I can't do anything for him or her anymore; I don't know what to say, what USE can I be?" is to miss the point. Anyone who stays with us even if we are wrong, who suffers with us in our predicaments without accusing us, without moralizing, anyone who is just there, is our friend.

This realization of what it means to be a true friend came to me through an experience I had some years ago.

We had a worker employed in our seminary in the Philippines who became very ill. People in the East always surround their sick ones with as many members of the family as possible in order to give him or her the feeling of closeness and care. They come and visit the sick person, not to do something or to say anything, but very often to be silently present, to suffer with him or her. They can sit there for hours without saying a word. The sicker the person becomes the more people might be present.

Having made up my mind to visit our worker and knowing that I am not a patient man, I resolved not to be the first to leave the hospital room. I went in and greeted the sick man who seemed to recognize me. The room was packed with people and terribly hot. Nobody said a single word. I sat down and waited. One hour passed - and a second hour and nobody got up to leave. My patience was running out and I regretted having made such a stupid resolution not to leave before anyone else. After ten more minutes a woman left. I got up after her, went to the sick man, prayed with him, and left.

Weeks later, I met the sick man now fully recovered and in good health. Full of surprise, I congratulated him on his speedy recovery. He said to me, "Father John, you will never realize how much your visit meant to me and how much it contributed to the fact that I am now alive and healthy. When I saw you coming all the way to visit me and to stay with me for two hours and ten minutes, I realized that people loved me and really wanted me to be well. I knew I had friends. In that moment, I started to fight my illness with all the strength I had left. I wanted to live because of you, because of my family, because of people who loved me and wanted me to be alive."

It is from this point of view that we have to look at the Bible and to see what it means to say our God is a GOD WITH US. He is a God who wants to be with us in our pain, miseries, loneliness, and anguish — situations where one can seemingly do nothing but just be there. He wants to console and comfort us with his unpretentious presence. We have to understand the God of the Bible from such a perspective or we will never know who he really is. It seems that God wants to know our human condition fully; he wants to suffer all our miseries and pains with us. He does not want to take them away before he himself has tasted them to the dregs. Our God is not simply an all-powerful God but a compassionate God. This is the real mystery of Revelation.

The compassionate God as revealed in Jesus Christ

The mystery of such a God has been revealed to us in the person of Jesus of Nazareth. He has revealed to us the mystery of God's compassion. In him it became visible. Jesus not only told us that we should be as compassionate as our Father in heaven is, but he made this divine compassion appear in our world in a concrete way.

All the actions and deeds Jesus performed were done out of compassion. The Hebrew word 'splangchna', used to describe Jesus' feeling compassionate, refers to the entrails of the body, the guts, the place where our most intimate and intense emotions are located. The word comes from the Hebrew word 'rachamin', which means a movement of the womb of God, the center of his being. In Psalm 51 we appeal to God's compassion, because in it lies our guarantee for forgiveness: IN YOUR GREAT COMPASSION, BLOT OUT MY SIN.

> Here the word 'compassion' or 'mercy' could actually be replaced by 'love'...according to your great love. The Hebrew word is 'ra-hammin', which means 'heart' or 'womb'. It is a very feminine or motherly term and denotes the ability to suffer with, to enter a situation deeply, to be filled with empathy, as if one is experiencing the situation personally and not as an observer. The word really means to be able to share the suffering and pain of others and also to experience their joy and happiness as if it was all happening to us. The word, as it is applied here to God, is comprehensible only to those who know what it means to love unconditionally, with all the fibres of their being, in total self-surrender and with passion. (adapted from Carlo M. Martini, *What am I that you care for me?*, *Praying with the Psalms*)

The compassion of God has been revealed in Christ's life and death. All the miracles Jesus did were done out of compassion. Twelve times do we find the word "compassion" in the Gospels used exclusively for Jesus and the Father. The most obvious places are the following:

Mt 18:23-25: The Parable of the Wicked Servant
The master felt compassion for him (v 27).

Lk 15:11-32: The Parable of the Lost Son
...his heart was moved with compassion (v 20).

Lk 10:30-35: The Parable of the Good Samaritan
His heart was filled with compassion (v 33).

In the Parable of the Lost Son, the father is shaken, moved in his inner being when he sees his son coming home. This being moved in his inner being becomes visible in Jesus. When Jesus sees suffering, pain and misery, he is shaken, he becomes part of it, he experiences the pain in his own heart and being.

Mt 14:14: When he saw the crowd his heart was filled with compassion.

Mk 1:40: When he saw the leper, he was moved with compassion.

Lk 7:13: When the Lord saw her, his heart was filled with compassion.

Whenever Jesus saw suffering people he was shaken, moved. He felt the depth of their sorrow. He felt it even more deeply than they could. It seems that he was sicker, hungrier, more sorrowful than they. It is here that the real depth of God's love is revealed. The true mystery of our God is not that he takes our pain and suffering away, but that he first wants to share them with us. Only when he has tasted them, experienced them, can they be changed; only then can new life come forth. The God of Jesus is not primarily an all-powerful God but a compassionate God. The really new in Jesus' message is that God is not a distant God, unmoved by our misery and pain, but a God who is WITH US, who is moved by our pain and misery, who participates in the fullness of our sin-permeated human condition, a God who is OUR GOD (Ph 2:6-8 he became obedient unto death). What is so unexpected and 'disturbing' is that God's compassionate love in Jesus is characterized by a downward pull. The whole life and mission of Jesus reveals that he, by accepting absolute powerlessness, shows the limitlessness of God's compassionate love for his creatures.

Compassion as revealed in Jesus is not a bending down towards the underprivileged from a privileged position. It is not a reaching out from on high to those who are miserable and below, it is not a gesture of sympathy or pity to those who have failed to make it. On the contrary, the compassion of God means that he moves directly to those people and places where suffering is visible and most tangible, and pitches his tent there, and does not turn back before having experienced himself all the misery, anxiety, loneliness, pain and suffering of the human race. God can be found most among the rejects, the outcasts, the marginalized. This is the real mystery of our God whom Jesus has revealed. God's unconditional love for us becomes, in a sin-permeated world, a compassionate love. It is a love that redeems the world by first suffering all the effects of our rebellion against God and then transforming the old into the new.

Jesus' death the ultimate proof of God's compassionate love

In the Incarnation, Jesus identified himself with us, although he did not sin. He took upon himself our situation, our state of broken existence. He entered a world of 'shell-people', people who had no basis to stand on, who were cut off from God and from each other. He wanted to experience this situation of being cut off from God and from others. He wanted to immerse himself totally in our situation to be one with us — Emmanuel. His life was ruled by two principles:

1.My food is to do the will of him who sent me (Jn 4:34). From the Father he drew his life; he was the rock on which he stood; to him he dedicated his whole life.

2.Total dedication to his mission, i.e., to us. No one has greater love than the one who lays down his life for his friends (Jn 15:13). He always loved those who were his own...now he showed how perfect his love was (Jn 13:1ff).

His mission consisted in drawing all human beings into that intimate loving relationship with God that he experienced so intensely in himself and which he expressed in the word "ABBA".

Jesus preached his message of God's love with great enthusiasm, and might have hoped that Israel would respond spontaneously and generously to the message. But very soon Jesus came to realize that Israel would not listen to his message. What should he do now? It became clear to him that the only way left to fulfill his mission was to demonstrate the immensity of God's love for us (Jn 13:1). The cross was the only way that remained to prove God's redeeming love in a sin-permeated history of humankind. Exegetes talk about a "Galilean Crisis" marking a turning point in Jesus' life. From Galilee on his attention is focused on his suffering and death in Jerusalem (Mk 8:28-31; 9:31; 10:33; 10:45).

Once Jesus comes to realize that the "will of the Father" is leading him to the cross to prove God's love "to the very end" for humankind, we do not find a man who frantically and fanatically runs towards the cross and his own death. Jesus is afraid and even horrified when he thinks of what is to come:

There is a baptism I still must receive and how great is my distress till it is over (Lk 12:50).

Now my soul is troubled. What shall I say: Father, save me from this hour? But it was for this very reason that I have come to this world (Jn 12:27).

In the days of his earthly life Jesus made prayers and requests with loud cries and tears to God to save him from death (Heb 5:7).

His sweat was like drops of blood falling to the ground (Lk 22:34).

At three o' clock Jesus cried out with a loud shout: My God, my God, why have you abandoned me (Mk 15:34).

What do these passages tell us? Was Jesus afraid of physical death? Here we can sense the tension between his intimate life with the Father and his "living our life to the very end", i.e., his faithfulness to his mission — identification and representation. First, **identification:** it seems Jesus felt that the more he identified himself with us, the more he would "experience" our sinfulness, our forlornness, our insecurity, the insecurity of those who had rejected God's gift of love as the only security for a creature. He came to realize that if he carried his mission through to the very end, he would have to experience the full reality of what it means for a creature to be "cut off" from the Father who meant everything to him, and from whom he drew life. The thought that this moment was coming horrified him. The Father would consider him as "humankind in its God-forsaken, abandoned state."

Second, **representation:** Jesus would have to experience this being completely IDENTIFIED with us in our sinfulness and being dealt with as our REPRESENTATIVE before God. The cry on the cross is the moment when Jesus identified himself most with our God-forsakenness (Mk 15:34). In this moment, it seemed as if the love of the Father, from which he drew life, had stopped flowing. God's compassion for his creature had reached the ultimate. Paul has expressed this in different ways:

God dealt with sin by sending his own son in a body as physical as any sinful body, and in that body God condemned sin (Rm 8:3).

Christ redeemed us from the curse of Law by being cursed for our sake (Ga 3:13).

For our sake God made the sinless one into sin, so that in him we might become the goodness of God (2 Co 5:17).

The cross is not the revelation of a revengeful God. It reveals two essential realities:

1. The immensity and incomprehensibility of God's compassionate love for his creature.

Compassionate love means God did not redeem the world by reaching down from on high but by "coming down" into our human misery and "loving it through" by experiencing it to the ultimate limits. In experiencing the effect of sin as condemnation, God took upon himself in Jesus Christ what would have been the destiny of a humankind that had rejected the very foundation of its existence — "He descended into Hell!"

2. The utter hopelessness of our human state, as sinners who had rejected God's love.

The cross tells us what sin really is. The death of Jesus, according to Mark 15:38-39, poses a few pertinent questions: Where can God be found? In the Holy of Holies? Mark tells us that at the moment Jesus died, the huge curtain that hung before the Holy of Holies was torn into two from top to bottom. What is Mark telling us? The Jews believed that God's foot touched the earth in the Holy of Holies. Here one could be sure to find God. The High Priest alone was allowed to enter this place once a year, and then only after fasting and prayer, because he would be standing before God. With the death of Jesus, God is no longer to be found in the Holy of Holies. It is empty. Everyone can now look into it. God has finally and ultimately revealed who he truly is in the death of his Son on the cross.

This is the most condensed and climactic revelation of God there is. For the Jews it is a scandal and for the pagans mere nonsense (1 Co 3:18). Who would ever have expected a God to reveal himself in this way — in absolute powerlessness, out of compassionate love for his creatures? God chose no other means to deal with his creatures than with love — and in order to save us he proved his love to the point of suffering our forlornness in order to redeem it. In the cry of this dying Jesus of Nazareth God has revealed his very nature, "How incomprehensible is God's love for us" (Ep 3:14-19). Who recognized Jesus on the cross as Son of God? Theologians? No, the pagan centurion!

No one has ever seen God. It is the only Son who is nearest to the Father's heart, who has made him known (Jn 1:18).

Yes, God loved the world so much that he gave his only Son... God sent his Son into the world not to condemn the world, but to save it (Jn 3:16-17).

The cross remains THE revelation of God's unconditional, compassionate love. Now it is possible to point to a visible, historically manifest fact, located in space and time and say, "Here is God's ultimate self-communication to us. God can never withdraw again."

To follow the compassionate Lord

The way we should love is forever explained in that phrase "AS I have loved you." This kind of love is not human. It is something we can only receive as a gift from God. The gift, however, is available, if we open ourselves to the Kingdom and let its power into our life:

Be compassionate as your Father is compassionate.

This will forever remain the guideline for all our relationships if we decide to enter into fellowship with Jesus. By putting our feet into his footprints and looking constantly at him and at how he revealed God's own compassion in his words and actions, we can gradually come to feel true compassion, and to love with compassion as he did. We will become compassionate people, and so will start acting as God acts. We will become like him.

Questions for Reflection:

1. Do I realize that God's powerlessness in the world is due to his compassionate love which cannot use power but only suffers with us before he can save us?

2. What rules my relationship with people, compassion or the law, which insists on right behavior and judges people accordingly?

TRUE FRIENDSHIP

"My friend isn't back from the battlefield, sir. Request permission to go out and get him."

"Permission refused," said the officer. "I don't want you to risk your life for a man who is probably dead."

The soldier went all the same and, an hour later, came back mortally wounded, carrying the corpse of his friend.

The officer was furious. "I told you he was dead. Now I've lost both of you. Tell me, was it worth going out there to bring in a corpse?"

The dying man replied, "Oh, it was, sir. When I got to him he was still alive. And he said to me, 'Jack, I was sure you'd come.'"

(Anthony de Mello, *The Prayer of the Frog*, Vol I)

3. Do I try to enter into other people's experience of joy, success, suffering, struggle, failure, or do I often look at others in a comparing, competitive way?

COMPASSION

Compassion manifests itself first of all in the consciousness of being part of humanity, in the awareness of the oneness of the human race, in the intimate knowledge that all people, wherever they dwell in time or place, are bound together by the same human condition. Through this inner sense of solidarity the even deeper bond with all of creation can be sensed. (H. Nouwen, *Compassion*)

4. How am I at this time being called to "empty myself" in order to live for and with others as Jesus did?

Story for Reflection:

WHERE IS GOD?

The three victims mounted together onto the chairs. Their three necks were placed at the same moment within the nooses."Long live liberty!" cried two adults. But the child was silent. "Where is God? Where is He?" someone behind me asked. At a sign from the head of the camp, the three chairs tipped over. Total silence throughout the camp. On the horizon, the sun was setting. "Bare your heads!" yelled the head of the camp. His voice was raucous. We were weeping.

"Cover your heads!" Then the march past the dead men began. The two adults were no longer alive. Their tongues hung swollen, blue-tinged. But the third rope was still moving; being so light, the child was still alive.... For more than half an hour he stayed there struggling between life and death, dying in slow agony under our eyes. And we had to look him full in the face. He was still alive when I passed in front of him. His tongue was still red, his eyes not yet glazed. Behind me, I heard the same man asking: "Where is God now?" And I heard a voice within me answering him: "Where is He? **Here He is — He is hanging here on these gallows...**"

(E. Wiesel, *Night*)

RELIGIOUS LIFE: FOLLOWING THE RADICAL LIFESTYLE OF JESUS

Introduction

Our essential vocation as Christians is to follow the Lord. This call is not something we can accomplish once and for all, as one finishes a project or task. No, to follow the Lord means to be always on the road, to become a disciple rather than to be one, to be always learning anew, never having reached the goal. We will always have to say with St. Paul:

> Of course, brothers and sisters, I really do not think that I have already reached it; the one thing I do, however, is to forget what is behind me and to do my best to reach what is ahead (Phl 3:13).

If following the Lord is the vocation of every Christian, where does religious life fit in? What is its special goal? How does it differ from the ordinary way of Christian life? Is this way of following the Lord a higher and a better way of following him?

I would like to begin with the description of religious life that emerged during the Second Vatican Council. The Council approaches religious life by examining its biblical roots. The two main aspects stressed by the Council are:

1. Religious life in terms of fellowship with Christ;

2. Religious life in terms of its ecclesial dimension as life IN and FOR the Church.

1. Religious life in terms of following and imitating Christ

The following of Christ is a call that concerns all Christians. It is something every Christen worthy of the name has to live out. Religious life follows this general call for all Christians.

Vatican II has made this very clear. The following and imitating of Christ is the cardinal occupation and pattern of life for all religious orders and communities. In Perfectae Caritatis 2, the Council states that the supreme law and fundamental norm for all religious life is the following of Christ as proposed by the Gospel. This is the essential nature of religious life in its classical definition, the standard by which everything else must be measured. What is it, then, that distinguishes this way of fellowship with Christ from the general call given to every Christian to follow him?

Many attempts have been made to answer this question and various proposals offered as a solution. Yet, when the literary dust has settled, most spiritual writers agree that it is the intensity and the radicalism with which one feels called to follow Christ and to imitate his radical life style that distinguishes religious life from the life of all the baptized. As the Council put it:

> The motive for entering religious life is to follow Christ more freely and to imitate him more nearly by the practice of the evangelical counsels (PC 1).

> Christ also proposed to his disciples that form of life which he, as the Son of God, accepted in entering this world to do the will of the Father. In the Church this same state of life is imitated with particular accuracy and perpetually exemplified. The religious state reveals in a unique way that the Kingdom of God and its overmastering necessities are superior to all earthly considerations (Lumen Gentium 44).

Radicalism seems to be the key-word. In the Gospel, one must recognize that there is a group Jesus chose from a wider group of followers to be his special disciples. They were to represent him to others in a particular way. The very fact that Jesus chose some among his followers to live with him on a more intimate basis set up a pattern of closer discipleship. This vocation to special discipleship is portrayed as a call to a life of sacrifice too severe to be generally acceptable (Mt 19:27; 8:19-20; Mk 10:21; Lk 9:23-24). Religious life is a response to this special call. It distinguishes itself, therefore, from ordinary Christian life in that it involves a call to commit oneself to the concrete life style adapted by Jesus when he walked this earth. Jesus did not make vows but he lived the content of the vows: he was poor, celibate and obedient.

Religious life is an invitation, i.e., a gift from the Lord to follow him in that radical lifestyle which he himself embraced. Those called are not better disciples than the ordinary followers of Jesus. This is only another way to follow him. Whether they become better disciples by following the invitation to live the radical lifestyle of Jesus is a different question. A religious is not automatically a disciple of Jesus because he is a religious. He or she might never succeed and may end up like the person described in Scripture.

> If one of you is planning to build a tower, he sits down first and figures out what it will cost, to see if he has enough money to finish the job. If he doesn't, he will not be able to finish the tower after laying the foundation; and all who see what happened will make fun of him. 'This man began to build but could not finish the job', they will say (Lk 14:28-30).

Religious life is specifically identified by the renunciation of three great human goods, a renunciation expressed by the vows of poverty, chastity and obedience. It is renunciation of three good things that, in principle, I could enjoy any time. I give them up for the Kingdom. But to see religious life only in terms of renunciation is too negative and too one sided. With Jesus a new reality, the Kingdom of God, has entered this world. This is a reality so concrete and so compelling in its attraction that there will always be people captivated by it. In the end such people can do nothing else but dedicate themselves totally and unconditionally to this Kingdom.

2. Origin of religious life in the Church

We know that religious life as we understand it today came into existence only in the fourth century. But there were some antecedents to it. In the early Church we already find people who wanted to follow the Lord in a more radical way by renouncing possessions and marriage in order to be closer in fellowship with him. They lived in their respective Christian communities. They gave witness that ultimately there can be no difference between being a disciple and being a Christian. While following the general call of the Christian they felt the Lord inviting them to a more radical way of being his disciples imitating his own chosen lifestyle.

The early Christian communities lived in a society which did not share their values. Therefore, they became automatically what Lohfink calls a "counter-" or "contrast society," witnessing to a different set of values and way of being human.

This situation changed dramatically when the Church became the state religion and people entered in droves. The Church ceased to be a counter-society. By conforming herself to society many felt that the Christian faith compromised itself. At that moment a new charism arose within the Church.

Actually it was not so much a new charism as a newly revived one, the prophetic charism of protest. Many scholars see here a remarkable resemblance to the beginnings of the prophetic movement in the ninth century BC when established Israel was forgetting to live in covenant love with her God and in justice and peace with each other.

John Cassian comments that the first religious went apart "to practice those things which they had learned to have been ordered by the apostles throughout the body of the Church in general" (Collationes XVIII, ch. 5). According to him, monks formed communities to see that these ideals be not just preached but lived. Religious life came into existence as a protest movement against a Church that had conformed itself too much to society at large. Religious life was seen as following the model of the prophets in the Old Testament (Fr. J. Moloney, *Disciples and Prophets*).

Many individual Christians at that time moved out into the desert and soon created new communities, which in turn took over the former mission of the Church to be a "counter-society." These communities patterned themselves on the community model of the early Church as described by Luke in Acts where everything was held in common by people of simple heart who called one another brother and sister.

Later other communities took their orientation from the group that had "followed Jesus when he walked this earth"; in short, the disciples of Jesus. The best examples are the communities founded by Sts. Francis, Dominic and Ignatius. Vatican II seems to have followed more this pattern in its description of religious life.

No matter which pattern one considers, that of a "counter-society" or radical discipleship, both seem to witness to the fact that there is always need within the Church for healing and a reminder of our basic call. In short, religious orders have a therapeutic task to fulfill for the Church. There seems to be a link between the Church's task to be a "counter-society" and the existence in the Church's history of monasteries and religious orders. Religious communities arose whenever the Church forgot or betrayed its essential task of following the Lord and was not offering to society at large itself as a "counter society".

It is not wrong to say that when the Church began to get sick, God ordained monks, nuns and cloisters as its therapy. When the Church forgot that it was to be a contrast society, a contrast society was created in its midst (G. Lohfink, *Religious Orders*).

The Mission of Religious Life

From a canonical point of view, the essential aspect of religious life is its focus on the three vows as they are described by each congregation in its respective constitutions. But the life of the vows is not something abstract, nor is the actual living of the vows always the same.

The concrete living of the life style of Jesus is largely determined by the work we do, by the circumstances of our daily lives. One fundamental difference is: St. Benedict, the father of monastic life in the West, moved into the desert to escape from a corrupt world. The founders of modern religious orders have moved straight into the corrupt world to proclaim and witness God's love there. This is a significant fact which influences the actual living of the vows.

If the essence of religious life is fellowship with Christ in a radical way, what then is its function? There is no calling in the Old Testament or in the New Testament that does not contain a mission. Any call is meant to engage one actively in the bringing about of salvation for the whole world.

The question I would like to raise and address here is: what is the essential function of religious life in the Church and in society at large, at the present moment? I would like to present three functions of religious life which seem to me to be essential for the present time.

1. to provide 'productive models' (INNOVATORY FUNCTION)
2. to play a 'corrective role'
3. to witness to community living

In the first two I will follow the thought of J.B. Metz (*Followers of Christ*).

a. The "innovatory function" of religious life

What does it mean to say that religious life has to fulfil an "innovatory function" for the Church? As was said earlier, all Christians are called to follow Christ and to carry on his saving mission. The difference between the general call of all and the call of religious was found in the radicalism to which the latter see themselves called.

The first mission or function of the religious life consists in providing a clear reminder of the intimate link between being a Christian and following

Christ. The general demand to follow Christ is too abstract. Its meaning and content have to be demonstrated by means of concrete models in every age and situation. The Church as a whole and society at large need patterns, models, visible forms which clearly and unmistakably reveal what the Gospel demand of following Jesus means today. In the Church this has always been seen as provided by the Saints.

Who can provide these new patterns or models? Metz sees that the role of religious life is to offer "productive models" for the Church as a whole. These models should illustrate how fellowship with Christ is to be lived in the new social, economic, intellectual and cultural situation of today. Following Christ is not just an application of the Church's Christology to our life. Who Christ is can never be known unless we enter on the way of following him. Following Christ can never be a purely spiritual endeavor. It has to be lived and demonstrated in the concrete circumstances of our time.

The attractiveness of Mother Teresa is precisely due to her way of following the Lord. She demonstrates clearly what it means to follow the Lord in the situation in which she works. This was the striking insight I gained when I worked with her group in Calcutta. For the first time I understood what following the Lord would mean in that situation.

To provide "productive models" means to show what being a disciple of Jesus is all about and to show what Jesus would do in the setting of our time, in a consumer society, in a world of massive injustice and abject poverty.

One may have different ideas about it, but the often heard "preferential option for the poor" comes ultimately out of the experience of what following Christ means in a situation that is marked by abject poverty and injustice. In such a world, fellowship with Christ, radically lived, leads the disciple to the poor, the rejected, and the marginalized of human society, who make up the greater part of humankind today.

The ones who have committed themselves to this kind of fellowship will help the Church to discover who Jesus is, and in him, who God really is. So the Church will discover that he is 'partial', i.e., that he is on the side of the poor and marginalized, and that his intention is to bring the Good News to them first. We cannot deduce this clearly and unmistakably from Scripture alone. It is only a concrete model of living the Gospel that can demonstrate to us today what the Gospel really tells us about God, fully revealed in Christ.

If we really want to know who the God of Jesus is, we might have to live his life, a life of total dedication to the poor and the marginalized. It seems to me that we are being stripped more and more of our wrong image of God through a purifying but painful process. Either we will discover God in the poor and oppressed or we will end up with no God at all.

It seems more and more obvious that the Latin American theologians were right. They told us ten years ago that there is no future for religious life unless religious take the option for the poor with absolute seriousness. Only in that commitment will we discover again what following the Lord today implies. In following him in this way, we will once again discover what kind of God it is who revealed himself in Jesus Christ. This we have to do not only for ourselves as religious but because we are called to fulfill a function in and for the whole Church.

b. The "corrective role" or the "shock therapy" of religious life

The constant danger of the Church as a large scale institution is accommodation and questionable compromise, i.e., the ever present tendency of making the Gospel livable in a consumer society by watering down its radicalism to the point that it does not hurt anymore. It is over against a too nicely balanced view of things and too much compromise with the standards of the time that religious life is seen as having to play a "corrective role."

The first religious moved out of society in protest against a Church that had accommodated herself too much to society at large and could not anymore be seen as a "counter society." She could no longer provide an alternative in the form of life the early Christians had chosen.

Religious life has a prophetic role to play in the Church and in the world. As such, it possesses a particular sensitivity to the signs of the times. After all, the prophets' task has always been to proclaim the will of God for today to the people of God. The function of the "prophetic role is, therefore, at times, to upset the so-called balanced view and so move the Church out of stagnated positions into new situations, to the frontiers, into new circumstances and challenges. Some theologians have proposed the same idea by seeing and understanding religious orders as "God's therapy for the Church" (N. Lohfink).

Why should this be their task? It is because religious congregations are the heirs and heiresses of great founders like Sts. Francis, Dominic, Teresa etc. These men and women upset the Church of their times by demonstrating the uncompromising nature of the Gospel, and by moving the Church, as an institution, into new situations and circumstances. This we have to do on the basis of our prophetic charism.

One of the greatest (and perhaps the most deadly) temptations of religious life is for religious to move too far towards the middle ground, where everything is nicely balanced and moderate, and to forget their prophetic vocation in and for the Church. Many religious do excellent work in institutions, but very often we have to admit that they fulfill a role society has assigned to them. They have been nicely integrated into society and are regarded as useful and appreciated for what they do. But they are also expected to stay there and not to move beyond the task assigned: to care for the old, serve in hospitals, run boarding schools, etc. They are not to meddle in any other ways with issues of society which often make or break human lives.

Surely, the "vocation crisis" vis-a-vis religious congregations has many roots. But at times I wonder, whether young people do see in religious orders any real alternative for a youthful and radical commitment. They instinctively feel that religious are just part of the system, giving it a charitable coat rather than presenting a contrasting community to a consumer society and challenging the most cherished ideas of such a society.

I am inclined to agree with a number of spiritual writers who see crisis of vocations in many religious congregations as linked to a "crisis of function." They no longer know what their specific role should be in the Church and the world. If it is correct to say that religious life in the Church is a prophetic ministry, then it is a matter of life and death that it remains constantly alert to fulfill its ministry by responding to the Spirit and moving to the frontiers where the Church has to implant itself anew.

Summary

The function of religious life follows logically from "the call" which is seen as an invitation "to follow the Lord more freely and to imitate him more exactly as he presents himself in the Gospel" (P.C. 2). To describe the function of religious life as "providing productive models" for the Church means nothing else than to say that religious should clearly and uncompromisingly demonstrate what they have committed themselves to in their vows. This means the willingness to follow the Lord more freely and to imitate him more exactly as he wants to be followed and imitated TODAY in our time and in our circumstances.

The mission of religious consists in showing through their own lives and actions who Jesus really is, what vision of God he proclaimed, lived, worked and died for; what vision of the world, human society, the individual person and creation as a whole he presented.

You might still remember the slogan that became so popular in the late sixties in the wake of the "God is dead" theology: "God is alive! I have seen a glimpse of him in you." Adapting this slogan to the function of religious life we could say that by looking at us, people should be able to say, "Christ is alive because I have seen a glimpse of him in you!"

The same holds true for the second function we mentioned, the "shock therapy" for the Church. Jesus at times vigorously protested against any compromise and accommodation of Israel's religion made by the religious leaders of his days. So it is our mission as religious, on the basis of our prophetic ministry, to act and to behave accordingly. That means we should have, first of all, a sense or a particular feeling for the compromises and the accommodations which the Church as a large-scale institution will always be tempted to make and does make with "the rulers of this world". Secondly, we religious ought to be highly sensitive to the signs of the times and be able to see with more clarity than others what kind of new situation the Spirit wants his Church to move into.

To illustrate the point, I like to use what may seem a strange comparison. Compare a religious with a cat. The cat's basic function is to be out catching mice. But a cat can also be a pet.It will look attractive with its glossy fur and it will purr nicely in the lap of its owner with the effect that it grows fat and lazy. Since its needs are taken care of, why should it catch mice? The same thing can happen to religious. They are meant to be out on the frontier, where things are not nicely settled and food is not always provided. Yet they can also let themselves be so easily integrated into the household of the Church and society that they become like fat and lazy cats, purring nicely, and being a mere shadow of what they were meant to be. In terms of their original function they are utterly useless. They have gotten so used to being provided for that they have forgotten what their real nature is.

We need to discover our true prophetic nature and to be alert to the signs of the times if we are to serve as "therapy for the Church" and society. If we fail to make use of this prophetic calling, God will have no use for us anymore. He will have to look for other movements to spread his liberating message in a way appropriate to the needs and circumstances of today.

This ought to be our mission, which we are called to live out and fulfill for the well-being of the Church and for its universal mission. It is given to us, not for our own glorification or for any kind of privilege in the Church. It is a charism to be exercised, so that the Church as a whole can fulfill its mission more faithfully. If we are to survive, the pattern of religious life must remain Jesus' own radical life style.

Our own frailty and imperfection should not hold us back from giving authentic witness to the Master whom we follow. He has assured us that we are HIS choice, poor as it is.

When our Lord went up to heaven after his resurrection one of the accompanying angels asked him:"Lord, who will carry on your work on earth?" Jesus, pointing to his disciples who were still standing down on the mountain from where he had departed, said: "These men down below, my disciples they will carry on my work." But the angels apparently not too impressed with this band Jesus had chosen as his messengers asked: "Just suppose they fail in their task, do you have another plan?" Jesus paused for a long time and replied: "No, there is no other plan, they are all I have to carry on my work."

The witness of community living

There is still one function left which many regard as vital for the mission of the Church today. This function should be exercised and lived out in particular by religious whose vocation is not to live as individuals but as communities. This function is the witness to community living.

Many spiritual writers say that religious life today must WITNESS TO COMMUNITY LIFE. Life in community must be a clear sign that our Christian faith can create communities in which peace, justice, love and true brother- and sisterhood are not just empty words, but lived realities. As communities within the Church, they serve as the visible and tangible anticipation of the final community which God intends for the whole of creation. The reconciling power of the Holy Spirit creates a community which, already here on earth, is to reveal that unity and harmony among men and women which is to find its fullness at the end of time. Because of all the brokenness of human life and the impossibility of ever creating any perfect community, the sign that God's Kingdom has broken into the world has to be demonstrated in our time.

This process of making the Kingdom initially present in our world is the task of the whole Church. But once again, religious communities should offer themselves as test cases, showing that the Kingdom has indeed already appeared in this world. In a time when people hunger after signs of God's Kingdom present, the question is: Who can give this witness to real community, if not the religious communities themselves? Who else can provide a more visible and tangible demonstration of the power of Christ's reconciling love in the Church as a whole if not religious communities, which claim to have made it their task to follow the Lord more freely and to imitate him more exactly?

Here once again the function of religious communities is to be a "counter-" or a "contrast society" for our time.

The importance of this appeal of religious life is being realized more and more. The Puebla Conference in 1979 listed four major concerns among religious:

1. the experience of God,
2. the witness to community living,
3. the preferential option for the poor,
4. the integration into the life of the local Church (726-738)

For many international congregations this has a special importance. Today all international congregations are seemingly moving towards a future where there will be no dominant nationality among them.

This has a true witness value. If we can demonstrate on the basis of our religious commitment that we can live in harmony and with brotherly and sisterly concern for each other, we offer an excellent witness to the power of the Kingdom already present for a world that desperately struggles to create a new international, social and political order.

Questions for Reflection:

1. Could someone looking at me recognize what genuine fellowship with Christ means today in the circumstances of life in which I live?

2. Am I aware of the "prophetic aspect" of my religious life, which calls me to engage myself in the task of helping the Church to adapt herself to new circumstances and situations - and not to compromise the Gospel for the sake of a false balance?

3. Are we witnesses to the community-creating power of the Holy Spirit in the sense that people by looking at us could say, "Look, how they love one another?"

4. Are we aware that religious life could well lead us today "Where we do not want to go?"

Story for Reflection:

A young man once dedicated his whole life to get to know the Deity whom he served. Year after year he intensified his prayer and fasting and did all kinds of ascetic acts with the sole aim of inducing the Godhead to disclose Himself to him. But to no avail. In his desperation he asked a pious monk what he should do.

The monk told him that there was a shrine somewhere in the mountains that was dedicated to the deity the young man served. If he would make a pilgrimage to this shrine the Deity would disclose himself to anyone who would ask.

The young man went off and he found the sanctuary. Here he prayed as he had never done before, days on end. Nothing happened. Just when he wanted to give up, the Deity spoke to him but without disclosing himself: "Return to where you came from, there is no answer for your request here because I have hidden my name in the very heart of your brothers and sisters. If you serve them you will find me."

(Legend told by Martin Buber)

To know Christ and to love him, that is our vocation but to succeed in this most necessary task of our life we will have to do both things: pray and serve our brothers and sisters.

FOLLOWING THE POOR JESUS: THE SPIRIT OF POVERTY

Introduction

The vow of poverty is the one vow that creates a lot of uneasiness, not to mention guilt, among many religious of our time. No one knows exactly how to define poverty or how to deal with it.

To use the word "poverty" sounds phoney as millions of people are faced with mass starvation, exploitation, oppression and misery. "We are not poor" is a phrase often heard from religious. We have plenty to eat, a roof over our head, a bed to sleep in. We are not powerless. We are not exposed to the frightening insecurity over what tomorrow might bring. All of these things are part of our experience. Therefore, we can hardly argue that we are poor.

In the face of such a dilemma, many would like to drop the word "poverty" and substitute another word like "equality," "detachment," or "availability." Others would like to return to a radical commitment to poverty as demanded by Jesus' command to the rich young man, "Go, sell all you have and give that money to the poor" (Mk 10:21).

Those who want to do this intend to make the word "poverty" credible to themselves and to the world in general. Whatever option one takes, the concept of poverty cannot be dismissed easily by anyone who calls himself or herself a disciple of Jesus. (Francis J. Moloney, *Free To Love*)

The life of poverty has a sound biblical foundation. It was part of Jesus' own experience and has always been part of the traditional structure of religious life. It seems to provide an answer to some of the deepest and most sincere questions posed by contemporary men and women, many of whom have come to realize that true freedom cannot be found in wealth and in possessions. The problem of poverty in the Church is old and new. This is shown by the following anecdotes.

A prelate once proudly showed St. Thomas Aquinas a large vessel adorned with precious stones. "Look, Master Thomas," he said, "now the Church no longer has to say, like Peter to the lame man at the Beautiful Gate (Ac 3:6), 'I have no silver and gold.'" "But," mused St.Thomas, "the Church also can no longer say the words immediately following, 'In the name of Jesus Christ of Nazareth, walk.'"

A medieval bishop looking at the Church as it existed around him, could find nothing of the poverty of Jesus and his disciples manifested in its institutions, saw nothing there of the paradox of the Sermon on the Mount, and nothing of the original poverty of the Jerusalem community. This led him to remark that every reading of the New Testament convinced him more and more that the Church of his time had a religion completely different from that of the Bible.

The problem of poverty is NEW in the sense that there is a dimension added to the vow of poverty which was not seen (or at least not stressed) in former times - the SOCIAL DIMENSION. Massive poverty as a global phenomenon, caused not by nature or calamity but by a particular world order, becomes the background over against which the vow of poverty is seen as including a "preferential option for the poor." This option is made in a Church which, as a whole, comes to realize more and more that "solidarity with the poor" is the only correct interpretation of Jesus' own "preferential love for the poor and marginalized."

No one can venture on the road today "to follow the Lord more freely and to imitate him more nearly" and leave out of his endeavor a conscious choice of a preferential option for the poor. Many of us, who decided to follow the Lord years ago, when this option for the poor was not so clearly stressed, might have to realize that the Lord is leading us today "where we would rather not go", namely, the way Jesus had to point out to Peter after Easter (Jn 21:18).

A correct understanding for our time of Jesus' central message of the Kingdom, by necessity, includes such a preferential option. Therefore, any serious renewal of our following and imitating of Jesus cannot talk about the vow of poverty and leave out the social dimension.

With the vow of poverty, as with all theological topics, the more it is discussed, the more it is necessary to go back to biblical roots. The first question is: what does Scripture reveal to us concerning poverty?

What does the Bible have to say about poverty?

The view of the Bible concerning poverty can briefly be summarized in three points:

1.THE POOR ARE THE PRIVILEGED OF GOD

God is on the side of the poor and oppressed and he is determined to restore their rights. God is not neutral, he is partial. "I have heard the cry of my people and I am determined to set them free from their slave-masters" (Ex 3:7-12; see also Ps 72: 12-14). Jesus took the same stand when he declared that God's Kingdom was first for those who society has marginalized (Lk 4:18ff).

2.MISTRUST CONCERNING RICHES AND POSSESSIONS

The Old Testament is ambiguous. Poverty was seen as a punishment; riches as a blessing. The history of Israel, however, proved that riches easily become a source of greed, injustice and unbelief. They create a false security found in possessions rather than in confidence in God. In the New Testament the issue is even clearer. The Kingdom of God is the only security there is and we cannot serve two masters (Mt 6:24). Possessions are seen as so fascinating and attractive that we easily take them as our ultimate security.

3.POSSESSIONS ARE FOR SHARING

The riches and possessions one has are not meant to be possessed selfishly and used simply for one's own comfort. They are in themselves good and not to be despised but are meant to be shared with one's fellow human beings. This was the basic view of the early Church (Ac 4:32-35).

Jesus' own lifestyle

When we come to the New Testament, we ask whether Jesus has anything to say about poverty? What did he expect from his disciples in this regard? The best way to answer these questions is to start off with the principles that ruled Jesus' whole life — total dedication to his Father and to his mission.

In letting himself be guided by these two principles, Jesus shows us not what it means to be God's Son, but, first of all, what it means to be truly human — to have no power, no support, no security except "the enthusiasm and commitment of one's own heart." (J.B.Metz, Poverty of Spirit) Jesus clung to nothing. "He did not count equality with God a thing to be grasped, but emptied himself" (Ph 2:6). This is most clearly displayed in the temptation story. The devil tempted Jesus to cling to his divinity, but Jesus refused. If Jesus had given in, the Incarnation would have become a divine puppet show. He rejected this temptation all his life. He never took refuge in his divinity in order to save his humanity.

His security, the rock he stood upon, was the knowledge that he was the beloved Son of the Father. This knowledge gave him the strength to risk being one of us. "Though he was rich, yet for our sake he became poor" (2 Co 8:9).

Jesus showed us what it really means to be human:

- to accept the givenness of life,
- the gratuitousness of creation,
- to acknowledge our poverty before God and
- to rejoice in it.

This was Jesus' own attitude. He lived out of that givenness of all things. He saw the world as it should be seen, created out of pure love and sustained by the Father's care. Mt 6:24-35 portrays in a beautiful way how Jesus looked at the world and the things surrounding him. The lilies in the field, the bird in the trees, all reminded him of his Father's love and care.

Poverty should help us to discover the beauty of creation. It should lead us to the realization that we exist because of God's unconditional love, a realization that should fill us with joy and thanksgiving. The secret of St. Francis' joyfulness consisted in his possessing everything without having anything. The rule of Taize puts it as follows:

The spirit of poverty does not consist in pursuing misery but in setting everything in the beauty of creation. The spirit of poverty is to live in the gladness of today.

Jesus did not develop an ideology of poverty. He could enjoy the things of this world without getting caught up in them. He was a free man, though he lived as a poor man. He expected those who would follow him to consider what would be in store for them. To one who wanted to join him Jesus said:

The foxes have holes and birds have nests but the Son of Man has no place to lie down and rest (Lk 9:58).

Jesus seems to be very hard on the rich.

"How hard it will be for rich people to enter the Kingdom of God." The disciples were shocked by these words, but Jesus went on to say. "My children, how hard is it to enter the Kingdom of God. It is much harder for a rich person to enter the Kingdom of God than for a camel to go through the eye of a needle." At this the disciples were completely amazed and asked one another, "Who, then, can be saved?" Jesus looked straight at them and answered, "This is impossible for humans but not for God; everything is possible for God" (Mk 10:23-27).

The utter amazement of the disciple is due to the general belief that riches were regarded as a blessing and as a sign of God's favor. Riches were believed to be definitely connected with the coming of the Kingdom. Why then was Jesus so hard on the rich? Why is it so "hard for them to enter the Kingdom?"

The Kingdom asks for a radical decision to leave all security behind and to put one's whole trust in the unconditional love of God. With this message Jesus entered the world. Riches carry the constant danger of making us rely on what we have and look for salvation from that source alone. Here again the most disastrous effect of original sin is clearly revealed - our desire to possess, to dominate, to make ourselves secure. In short, to have something to offer, rather than accept God's love and to admit joyfully that I live only because of his love. Is not ultimately the desire to have, to accumulate, to hoard, the real cause of the massive poverty and oppression that we see around us today?

Poverty, by stripping us of all the false facades that we use to buttress an insecure sense of self, enables us to be simply who we are and to receive God's gratuitous love as unearned gift. Paradoxically, this child-like simplicity takes a lifetime to achieve. As human beings, we are so radically beset by self-doubt about our essential goodness and value that we are constantly fortifying a weak self-worth by identifying with "other things." These things are of infinite variety. They can be our looks, talents, degrees, possessions, reputations, careers, performance and even our health. We glory in these things that seem to bolster our worth. As Christians we must separate ourselves from these things that conceal the real self. This letting-go process allows us to enjoy a peaceful kind of freedom in our relationship to the material world. We can be at peace in having or not having. (Wilkie Au, *By Way of the Heart*)

However, Jesus was not a fanatic. Since he was free from the desire to possess, he could enjoy the things of this world. He ate with the wealthy of his time and let himself be invited into their homes (Lk 5:29; 7:36). There were plenty of women in his company who served him.

> With him were the twelve as well as certain women who had been cured...Mary surnamed Magdalene, Johanna, the wife of Herod's steward Chuza, Susanna, and several others who provided for them out of their own resources (Lk 8:2-3).

Jesus let himself be anointed by a woman with "most expensive ointment", which she poured on his head.

> "Why wasn't this ointment sold for three hundred denarii and the money given to the poor" (Jn 12:4-6) (Judas who asked this question). When his disciples saw this they were indignant. "Why this waste?" they asked. "This could have been sold at a high price and the money given to the poor" (Mt 26:6-10).

Here again Jesus is free. He realized that the true motive behind the woman's deed was sincere gratitude and love. So we can understand his indignation at the disciples' reaction.

The fact that you can never please everyone becomes clear in this incident:

> What description can I find for this generation...For John came, neither eating nor drinking and they say 'he is possessed.' The Son of Man came, eating and drinking and they say, 'Look, a glutton and a drunkard, a friend of tax collectors and sinners' (Mt 11:16-19).

Yet, there is no doubt that Jesus himself lived as a poor man and constantly portrays a preferential love for the poor and for those we call today the marginalized.

The spirit of poverty and discipleship

Since it seems impossible today to present a unified view on poverty and a clear outline as to how the vow of poverty has to be lived in our time, different models of poverty have been worked out by spiritual writers. Each model tries to portray the vow of poverty from a particular aspect. The models are not exclusive. In fact, they complement and correct each other. The difficulty of defining poverty does not consist in the attitude that moves one to make the vow of poverty but rather in the functional aspect of this vow, i.e., how we have to live poverty in our daily work and apostolates.

What is most important is that we always keep in mind that poverty ultimately concerns our living relationship with the Lord whom we want to follow. The vow of poverty is the result of that relationship and only a means of expressing and developing this relationship. Discipleship is our call and essential vocation. The vow of poverty is based on the desire to follow the Master and to pattern our life after him. Like his poverty our vow is concerned with loving God, all human beings and creation at large. Only secondarily is poverty concerned with things, and the 'thingness' of poverty means nothing unless it expresses this one great love which is at the heart of all reality.

The experience of God's unconditional love which came into this world with Jesus provides me with a security, an Amen, that makes me forego any worry about my security in this world. It is reliance on God alone which is the basis for this vow of poverty. It is the attempt to follow Jesus' life-style that provides the inspiration to leave everything and to follow him in this way (Mk 10:21). It expresses the wish to be poor out of the desire to be one with Jesus, who had nothing on which to lay his head (Lk 9:58), and who emptied himself to become human (Ph 2:6-8). It is the desire to live as truly authentically and humanly as Jesus lived: to have no power, no support, no security, except "the enthusiasm and commitment of one's heart" (Metz). Or, in the words of the IMITATION OF CHRIST, one wants to live out the life motto of so many saints: *Nudus nudum Jesu sequi* — to follow naked the naked Jesus. "The hero is sheathed in armor, the saint goes naked." His or her only protection is friendship and union with Christ.

At times we need to experience ourselves how much we, who have made a commitment to follow the poor Jesus, lose our freedom and become dependent on what become "necessities" in our lives. Before I went to the Philippines, I packed all my belongings into seven big boxes and shipped them from Italy to Manila. When they arrived a year or so later, I opened them only to find myself facing a very unpleasant surprise. Everything had been stolen. The boxes had been stuffed with stones wrapped in paper. All I found was one sock. It literally took me weeks to get over that shock. Gradually I realized how attached I had become to many conveniences, and for the first time, I had a new understanding of my vow of poverty. I even managed to ask the Lord to bless the thief, because it dawned on me that he or she had actually done me a favor. In memory of this liberation I had undergone, I nailed that one sock into my closet as a thankful reminder.

There are two incidents in the life of St. Francis which are indicative of his spirituality and which portray with clarity this call to his followers to 'follow naked him' who divested himself of all he possessed for our sake. The first incident occurred at the beginning of his conversion when he took off all his clothes in the market place of Assisi and laid them at the feet of his father. The second occurs at the end of his life, when he asked his companions to strip him naked and to lay him on the bare ground, as he wanted to die that way. Uttering the words, "Brothers, now let us finally begin." Francis had at last rid himself of "all armor".

What counts and must have the primacy is people. Poverty, voluntarily chosen, liberates me from any obsession to make myself secure and frees me from the danger of treating people according to what they have. Poverty helps me to respect every person in the same way and to grow in love for each one.

Gandhi once said,

"It was only when I made the vows of poverty and chastity that I was able to treat all people equally."

Or, as Vincent de Paul put it,

"The poor will never forgive you the good you do to them, if you don't love them."

This is the true basis for the vow of poverty. If this basis is missing, this vow has no value. After all, we do make this vow only because we want to follow the Lord more freely and imitate him more exactly. Jesus has to remain the point of orientation whenever the question is asked as to how we should live this vow today in our time and setting. The vow of poverty, therefore, should enable me four things:

1. To lead me to a true commitment to follow the Lord in this radical way, to tie me more closely to him. This is really the essence of such a vow. After all, I make this vow to follow him in a radical way.

2. To realize the givenness of life and the gratuitousness of creation and to rejoice over it.

3. To free me from the disastrous effects of Original Sin — the desire to have, to possess, to dominate and to make myself secure.

4. To free me for people, to realize that all are equal and are the highest good there is, to dedicate myself to them, to have time for them.

This is what we could call the SPIRIT of poverty which Jesus lived so radically and to which he invited all who would follow him.

Questions for Reflection:

1. How truly can I say that 'the enthusiasm and commitment of my heart' are my only power, support and security?

2. How constant an attitude is gratitude in my life?

Story for Reflection:

HOFETZ CHAIM

In the last century, a tourist from the States visited the famous Polish rabbi, Hofetz Chaim.

He was astonished to see that the rabbi's home was only a simple room filled with books. The only furniture was a table and a bench. "Rabbi, where is your furniture?" asked the tourist. "Where is yours?" replied Hofetz. "Mine? But I'm only a visitor here. I'm only passing through," said the American. "So am I," said the rabbi.

When a man begins to live more deeply within, he lives more simply without.

(P. J. Wharton, *Stories and Parables*)

FOURTEENTH CONFERENCE

DIFFERENT MODELS OF POVERTY

Introduction

We have talked about the spirit of the vow of poverty, a spirit based on the desire to follow the lifestyle of Jesus more radically and to live as he lived. He lived out of that total trust in the Father's love for his creatures in which we find our security and which is the foundation on which we stand. We have to keep in mind that each vow is a love gift, a call from the Lord to "be with him" and to "be sent out" (Mk 3:13-15). The intention of this gift is to move us closer to him and to enable us to carry on his mission more faithfully. Without this spirituality the vow is empty. In our daily life, however, we have to give flesh to this vow and live it apostolically. Several models have been worked out in order to show how we should look at this vow. These models are not exclusive; in fact they complement and correct each other. (G. R Grosh, *Models of Poverty*).

Poverty as "community sharing"

We know that the earliest religious communities patterned themselves on the community model of the early church as described by Luke in Acts where everything was held in common by people of simple heart who called themselves brother and sister. They did not talk much about poverty. All Luke has to say is that "there was not a needy person among them" (Ac 4:34). Later other communities took their orientation from the group that had "followed Jesus when he walked this earth"; in short, the disciples of Jesus. The best examples are the communities founded by Sts. Francis, Dominic and Ignatius.

Community sharing seems to have been the basic pattern for the vow of poverty right at the beginning of religious life. At the moment it is gaining new emphasis among spiritual writers (F. Molony, *Free to Love*). As religious we not only live and work together, we also share our material goods. This model of the vow points to the fundamental unity which we have as religious: a unity in Christ. The basic premise is our shared life in Christ. We are a new creation, a new existence, a new being in Christ. The particulars that separate us have disappeared. Those who have been baptized "into Christ," who have "put on Christ," are all one in him.

> As a result, there are no Gentiles and Jews, circumcised and uncircumcised, barbarians, savages, slaves, or free men but Christ is all, Christ is in all (Col 3:11).

> So there is no difference between Jews and Gentiles, between slave and free man, between men and women; you are all one in union with Jesus Christ (Ga 3:28).

These texts have been given different interpretations even in our time. While the texts clearly declare that all privileges and advantages derive from legal positions and as such are made null and void because of our unity in Christ, the exegetical interpretations given to these texts are not that clear. Many protestant exegetes have understood the texts in the following way: There is, at least, one place in this world where all differences are annulled and done away with and that is when we are gathered together to worship and listen to the word of God. At that very moment and only then, there is no difference anymore, and the texts find their fulfillment. But the moment we leave the realm of worship and return to our daily lives, this old world with its own structures and classifications takes over again.

The vow of poverty seeks to abolish such a wrong interpretation of the Kingdom's presence in this world. To be "in Christ" means to live in a new situation, in a new environment, in a set of new relationships, a new sphere of existence. To be a Christian means to go away from one place to another place where the normally-accepted barriers between persons are brushed aside. Christian life, at its root, means a shared life, i.e., we depend on each other and others depend on us. Poverty here is seen from this basic premise:

> All the believers were of one heart and soul and no one felt that what he owned was his own; everyone shared...There was no one in the group who was in need...and the money was distributed to each one according to his need" (Ac 4:32-35).

The sharing here is a sign of love which each member of the community has for the others, especially those most in need. They share on the basis of their new life in Christ. The pagans did not say, "See how they hand in their goods," but, "See how they love one another."

The immediate effect of this shared life is that everyone, including the wealthy, now depends on the community for his or her well-being. The sharing of material goods becomes the expression of that mutual interdependence and sharing at the deeper level of "life in Christ", which is the basis of an authentic Christian existence and of the freedom of humanity.

The vow of poverty expresses a profound desire in us to share all that we have and all that we are because of the unique experience of our faith in Jesus. Poverty proclaims not the evil of possessions but the value of shared life, inspired by the radical faith demanded by Christ. The essence of poverty is the sharing of a new life in Christ.

This view of poverty as community-sharing, based on our unity in Christ, addresses itself to the call of the Kingdom which is in some way present now and which demands of us that we build the new society of the future Kingdom now within the conditions of the old society. The old society is a world in which the most disastrous effect of sin is the tendency to possess, to create our own security by having more, to compete, to get ahead of my fellow human beings, to "make it" in a competitive society where only the strong survive.

This view of poverty constantly raises the question as to whether or not the idea of a "new society" in terms of "community-sharing", based on our new life in Christ, is a little too utopian? It is true that on the basis of purely human endeavor, it does not seem possible. On the basis of our faith in the new life in Christ, however, it IS possible, though it will never be perfect, since it will always be marked by our own sinfulness. But in the measure we succeed, we are witnessing to the "new society" and at least to the tiny beginnings of the Kingdom present in this world now. Our witness of "community-sharing" becomes, therefore, a sign of the Kingdom present in this world, visible to those who can see.

In a world that can survive only if we share the goods of the earth, a reality that becomes clearer every day, the genuine witness of community-sharing is all the more important. By our living poverty, by sharing all that we are and all that we have, we may produce a quality of community life that makes people stop and wonder. We could then become a model of how society at large must be restructured if the principles of the Kingdom present are taken seriously. This would fit in perfectly with what we said earlier: that one of the main priorities of religious life today seems to be the witness it has to give to community living.

This model of poverty not only demonstrates the new unity based on Christ, the new society of justice, peace and joy in the Holy Spirit as the true future of humankind (Rm 14:17), it also helps us to overcome our inborn tendency to possess, to rule and to have more. Thus the vow of poverty is meant to free us from this disastrous effect of original sin by setting us free for love. Viewing poverty as community-sharing, however, must be supplemented by other models. Inherent in this model is the danger that it might induce the members to close in on themselves as long as they share what they have, and so they become blind to what is going on in the world that surrounds them. This model alone seems to me to be too narrow to cope with the issues we have to face today. Here the social dimension of poverty can be of great help.

> Spiritual poverty does not necessarily require being in destitution, or neglecting to provide for the future. It means simply that our resources are not amassed in order to establish an arrogant self-sufficiency, but are allotted in a planned manner to enhance our relationship with God and others. (Wilkie Au, *ibid.*)

The vow of poverty as "poverty of life"

This model focuses on the actual life-style of the individual members. Most constitutions start with this aspect, saying that poverty means to adapt Jesus' own simple way of life to the circumstances of our time. Every individual member is asked to examine his or her own life-style and to remain honest in terms of what one spends. In the face of the enormous problems of poverty in the world, one must ask: How does my life-style compare with that of millions of poor people? Can I justify my expenditure on clothing, living standard, travel and recreation? Here each one of us, as well as every community, will have to enter into a process of self-evaluation in terms of our ability to live more simply and with less.

The danger, however, is that we might fall into a subjectivism that leads to narrow-mindedness and even stinginess in considering the justified needs and wishes of the individual members and of the community. It can easily lead an individual to become judgmental, using his or her standard as a measure for everyone in the community. If this model is going to work, each community will have to work out some reference point that is external to the community. Many religious communities, for example, have used the average earnings of an ordinary worker in the country in which the religious lives as such a standard. So the concrete question each member of the community has to ask is: How does my lifestyle compare with that of the average worker in the country I live in?

> We live in a culture of achievement and production which believes that people should and do get what they deserve. As Christians we know that

this is not so. The infinite bounty of God begins with the gift of life itself and continues with everything that sustains it. Our activity is not so much an earning our way as a cooperating with the Creator God in transforming history into God's reign of justice and love...The capacity for enjoyment, for the sharing of simple pleasures, for delight in uncontrived beauty, has to be developed in our artificial and overstimulated environment. But these are essentially contemplative attitudes that conduce to recollection of spirit and prayer and that bathe our surroundings in evangelical poverty (Sandra M. Schneiders, *New Wineskins*).

Poverty as availability

A wider dimension of poverty, more than that which merely involves material goods, is being given more emphasis today. According to this concept, poverty is seen as functional, as being in the service of others. One has to be poor and free for total self-giving in order to be at the disposal of others.

There are three things each individual possesses: TIME, ENERGY and TALENTS. All one has and all one needs is seen to be for the service of others. Our apostolic service determines the things we need. This model allows great flexibility and adaptability and is the one most religious agree on. For myself, I like it best. It asks for a real detachment from material things, if it is going to work. The question to be asked constantly is: Do I really need this or that for my apostolic service?

This model thus needs constant discerning and a genuine spirit of detachment. Otherwise, one could justify everything in the name of apostolic service — expensive trips, vacations, expensive equipment, cars and hobbies. All this is easily justified by saying, "I need these things in order to be more effective in my ministry."

This model of poverty puts the stress on my availability. People are what counts. Do I have time for them? Do I treat everyone equally? Are people important, not on the basis of what they have, but on the basis that they are persons?

Another question I must ask myself is, "HOW DO I USE MY TIME?" Do I measure out the amount of time I give each day in the service of the Kingdom? How zealous am I really? Do I do my share to secure the livelihood of the community in which I live or do I just take without ever bothering to give in return?

As communities, we have houses, properties and equipment we need for effective apostolic work. The question we constantly have to ask is: Are we willing to make our community facilities available to other people and not just keep them for ourselves? What we have was given for the apostolate. We should not forget that.

When it comes to acquiring new equipment or buildings, the question should not be: Do we really need this or that? Rather, can we do without it? This question becomes all the more important in the light of the situation in which we live today.

A student approached the Teacher with a question. "When Jesus told the man to sell all that he had and give it to the poor, did he mean that we must get rid of everything?"

The Teacher answered with a story: "Once there was a man who listened to the Scripture. One day he heard Jesus quoted as saying to the rich man, "Go! Sell all that you have, give to the poor, and you will have riches in heaven, and come follow me."

The man stiffened. This was a word to him for he, like the rich man, was seeking salvation. First, he sold his car. After he gave the money away, he again listened, and heard Jesus say, "Sell all!"

Next he sold his house. After he gave the money away he listened again, and heard Jesus say, "'Sell All!"

"All that he had left was his Bible, which he sold for a few dollars. When he gave the money away, he again listened. This time he heard nothing."

The student said, "Teacher, I don't understand this story. Why did the man hear nothing?"

The Teacher answered, "He heard nothing because he sold the one thing that brought him the voice of God. We are not asked to rid ourselves of those things that draw us close to the heart of God. Jesus told the man to sell everything because his possessions were an idol. We must rid ourselves of whatever stands in the way to God. Now you must decide whether the things you own bring you close or separate you from God."

Poverty as a "visible aspect" (social aspect of poverty)

We experience today a greater sensibility to the abject poverty of millions of people. This model of poverty is linked to the burning issue of social justice and the creeping disease of consumerism. Living standards and levels of consumption are, of course, relative. What might constitute frugality here or there, might be regarded as opulence in other areas. The social model thus calls for a re-examination of the lifestyle of the community in the light of these issues.

The really difficult question is: How can we live a visible witness as community? As individual members we do not have much. Compared with the poor, however, we are not really poor. There is plenty to eat, a roof over our heads, a bed to sleep in. We are secure. In short, we have all the necessities of life, without real worries.

The individual cannot live out this model alone, because he or she has no decisive say in the community's possessions. If we do concentrate on living out this model of poverty, it can only be done in conjunction with a community discernment process whereby an individual community starts ridding itself of many things (buildings, property etc.) which all agree can be dispensed with. This model remains the great challenge to us today. One cannot set it aside without having gone through the process of community discernment. The visible witness of poverty needs to be lived because today, more than ever, it seems that "the way of doing things is more important for witness than the things we do" (P. Arrupe, S.J.).

> It is not easy to work out what the vow of poverty means in today's world. In principle, it means to participate prophetically in the human efforts to convert the race from exploitation to responsible stewardship, to liberate the poor by an equitable distribution of goods, to create the economic structures which will effectively relate finite resources to human ends. But it also means to model a sharing of life through a sharing of goods that expresses a Christian experience of poverty of spirit. In the concrete it probably means a re-evaluation of holdings and lifestyles and an abandonment of the privatized exclusivity of the religious subculture. To work out the details of such an approach will not be easy. But a poverty of this kind, which renounces both the childish irrelevance of an artificial dependence and the romanticism of a useless and unreal imitation of the destitute and concentrates on alleviating misery while building the structures of human solidarity, can make sense to the religious who vows poverty today. And although the world will undoubtedly not always like what religious are doing in this area, it will at least have to take it seriously. (Sandra M. Schneiders, *ibid.*)

Poverty as "preferential option for the poor" or as union with the poor and exploited (social dimension)

The vow of poverty is regarded in this model as a commitment to the plight of the poor. It can be said, that "a sharpened sensibility to injustice and oppressive structures at all stages might be considered the greatest single mental change that is taking place." Yet, how deeply it will affect people's spirituality is hard to say. At times one is amazed at how much resistance to this view there still is. The milieu in which we live can very easily insulate us from the simple life and its everyday concerns. Familiarity with poverty and misery can easily blunt awareness. Nor does mere awareness lead to solidarity with the poor. The close link we often have with the system that is largely the source of the misery of the poor can prevent us from standing up and speaking out. We either keep silent or we do not want to see.

I came across an example of this attitude in Latin America when I visited a classmate of mine who really does excellent work in his parish. While visiting some of his parishioners who were working in a limestone pit located in his parish, I asked him whether he was aware of what these men were paid. One of the workers had told me what they received for their ten hours work a day. He said he did not want to know because he didn't want to get involved in that. "After all, their bosses are the ones who make the parish run," he said.

Only a constant process of "conscientization" and a critical analysis of the socio-political situation in which we live can open our eyes to the plight of the poor and oppressed. Many tell us that we will never really commit ourselves to the preferential option for the poor if we continue to live in a world in which we feel secure and comfortable. What is needed is our insertion into the life of the poor. Without such an insertion, at least for a time, it seems almost impossible for this preferential option to become a conversion that will allow one to see the world through the eyes of the poor and to read the Bible accordingly.

If we make this option for the poor a priority in our lives, it will take a long and painful process of conversion. In case we decide on that road, we should take the risks into account. We will become controversial, we might be called leftists, and we could even lose our benefactors. It might mean that we lose our security and plunge into numerous uncertainties. Father Pedro Arrupe once said,

> When this happens to us, rejoice. This will be an encouraging sign that our solidarity with the poor is authentic.

The preferential option for the poor cannot remain an exotic endeavor of a few enthusiasts. Jesus' own preferential love for the poor demands of us today, if we really analyze the socio-political situation of the world, a commitment to engage in the creation of a world where the poor and the oppressed can once again experience what the Kingdom of justice and peace is all about. To do this we need a strong spirituality that orients itself constantly to Jesus' own preferential love for the poor. This way will certainly lead us "where we might not like to go" (Jn 21:18). It will not only determine our entire missionary and pastoral work, but also how we give expression to our vows of poverty, chastity and obedience today.

In a world where millions struggle for survival and many never succeed in obtaining the minimum of this world's goods voluntary poverty is probably the most convincing sign of our **vacancy for God**. It might sound common place, but it is true: **wherever the Church is vital, it is poor.**

Wherever the Church renews itself,it embraces voluntary poverty as a spontaneous response to the situation in this world, a response that expresses criticism of the growing wealth of the few and solidarity with the growing misery of the many. (H. Nouwen, *Clowning in Rome*)

Conclusion

These models of poverty, as we said in the beginning, have to be seen as complementary. They can act as correctives to one another. Many spiritual writers still put the stress on the first model, that of community-sharing on the basis of our unity in Christ. Everyone will have to examine his or her own view. But in the setting of our missionary vocation, there are some models that correspond better to the present situation than others. Poverty today seems to include, first, a strong call to a much simpler lifestyle, even a radically simple one, in the context of the burning issues of our time, and second, a preferential option for the poor.

Questions for reflection:

Each individual and each community (taking the particular situation into consideration) might have to examine themselves on these issues:

1. What is my view (our common view) of poverty? Which models do I (we) hold and favor?

2. How do I (we) live poverty concretely?

3. How can I (we, as community) give witness to poverty in the situation in which I (we) live?

Story for Reflection:

INNER FREEDOM

The sannyasi had reached the outskirts of the village and settled down under a tree for the night when a villager came running up to him and said, "The stone! The stone! Give me the precious stone!"

"What stone?" asked the sannyasi.

"Last night the Lord Shiva appeared to me in a dream," said the villager, "and told me that if I went to the outskirts of the village at dusk I should find a sannyasi who would give me a precious stone that would make me rich forever."

The sannyasi rummaged in his bag and pulled out a stone. "He probably meant this one," he said, as he handed the stone over to the villager. "I found it on a forest path some days ago. You can certainly have it."

The man looked at the stone in wonder. It was a diamond.

Probably the largest diamond in the whole world for it was as large as a man's head.

He took the diamond and walked away. All night he tossed about in bed, unable to sleep. Next day at the crack of dawn he woke the sannyasi and said, "Give me the wealth that makes it possible for you to give this diamond away so easily." (Anthony de Mello, *The Song of the Bird*)

PRAYER FOR THE GIFT OF POVERTY

Lord Jesus, I ask you for a new fullness of the charism of poverty. I ask you to reveal to me my inordinate attachments, my holding on to things or to persons, my 'richness' that keeps me from saying a more complete yes to you.

I surrender to you my excessive search for material comforts, and whatever material goods I have that I do not really need to serve you.

I surrender to you my excessive need for attention, for acclaim and applause. I surrender all my selfish ambition, my search for honors, my vainglory and my pride.

I surrender to you my possessiveness of those whom I love. Teach me to love freely, leaving others free, teach me to love with an open hand. Teach me to love more and better.

Give me the interior poverty that depends on you and not on the world's acceptance. Teach me to enter by the narrow gate that leads to life. You are that gate, Lord, let me follow you, taking up my cross.

For you alone, Lord, are my portion. I have no inheritance, for you are my inheritance; I want no possessions, for you are my possession (Ez 44:28).

Amen.

(Robert Faricy)

OPTION FOR THE POOR: CHANGE IN VALUES

Introduction

I have talked about the vow of poverty and the various models that we encounter today, I would like to further broaden the scope of the topic and reflect on a term mentioned more and more in the context of a committed Christian life, i.e., the "preferential option for the poor." This option places the vow within the concrete situation of our contemporary world. In their general chapters over the past ten to fifteen years, most religious congregations and orders have made the "preferential option for the poor" or the "promotion of justice and peace in solidarity with the poor" their top priority. However, those who have been appointed as animators to promote this option at the grassroots of our congregations are sometimes amazed at how much resistance they encounter when it comes to implementing the consequences of such an option.

Why do some of our members react with such resistance? Is the issue not clear, or is this understanding of the Gospel too reductionistic or one-sided? Is it only a fad that will soon fade, or was choosing it as a priority a complete mistake? What is it that causes many religious, otherwise highly-dedicated members of our congregations, to feel so threatened when this topic comes up?

The answer is not a simple one. While the above mentioned reactions may contain some value, we have to probe a little deeper. Is it selfishness or fear?

I am not saying that people who find the demand for a preferential option on behalf of the poor so difficult are more selfish than those who make such a commitment. There are more general reasons which we have to explore. One of the main obstacles confronting a more active engagement or commitment to the poor is the feeling that we are trapped by decisions which we ourselves did not make. A sense of GUILT and POWERLESSNESS penetrates our whole being. What can we do in the face of such immense problems? Charles Elliott has outlined this in his book "Praying the Kingdom". Although this book addresses itself primarily to First World Christians, it concerns each one of us. None of us can escape its pointed questions. For Elliott the trap operates as follows:

Guilt feelings

First, looking at the situation of certain people with open eyes, I soon come to realize that in comparison I am rich and they are poor. Somehow I feel that I am co-responsible for this state, since it is created, maintained and defended in my name as well, and with my tacit approval.

Secondly, whether I like it or not, I benefit from this state of affairs. I could not do what I am doing and maintain my lifestyle if things were different.

Thirdly, my life reflects a value system and style of thought that are inconsistent with both love of God and love of the poor. I become part of a process whereby values, ways of looking at the world, mindsets become embedded in our political and social culture. I am trapped because I am human and, moreover, I am human in our society at this particular time.

In short, we could say the common form of guilt manifests itself in a sense of being caught up in a system that is penetrated by sin to its deepest level while one draws benefits from the same system.

Powerlessness

The frustration I feel is based on the fact that I know injustice and denial of the Kingdom are built into our political life and I can do nothing about it: I feel utterly helpless. The reaction to these feelings of guilt and powerlessness is often verbalized as follows:

"I, at least, want to DO something since I cannot live with these feelings all the time." But instead of facing these feelings directly I can opt for cop-outs as a safety device. These can take the following forms:

OVERINDIVIDUALIZATION OF RELIGION. I concentrate on myself and block out the world: in my religion I focus on my personal relationship with God, my state of grace, my progress along the spiritual path. By doing so, I successfully opt out of the difficult task of getting involved in something I feel so helpless about. This is a tendency found among a number of religious. I stick to the old proven ways of spirituality and find my peace and tranquility there.

A second cop-out is HYPERACTIVISM. To compensate for my guilt, fear and powerlessness, I fall into a kind of manic activity. It helps me forget, and at least gives me the feeling I am doing something.

Privatization and hyperactivism can produce a tendency to project some of the unresolved conflicts on others: multinationals, military, industrialists and financiers, etc. This escape is a great temptation for people living in Third World situations or being of the Third World. It easily excuses me from taking a hard look at myself and how I am caught in a lifestyle that is contrary to what I actually proclaim.

A third cop-out is SUBSTITUTION. My time and my energy are limited, so I choose some endeavor I can handle and get busy in. The danger is that for the greater glory of God, I become excessively concerned with the trivial since I have a constant need for insulation from the horror of the world.

A possible solution

None of these cop-outs are a solution: the problem still remains to be solved. The direction to move in searching for a solution can be found basically by doing two things:

First, I must achieve an honest awareness of the object of guilt without any attempt to escape. Secondly, I must discover the myriad ways in which I am married to the system and begin freeing myself from these bonds. The issue is a question of values. Our values are unconsciously linked to the system in which we feel ourselves trapped. In order to change our values we have to be exposed to new situations, to discover for ourselves new values and so come to acquire a different vision of reality. We cannot impose values. If we do, people will resist. We ought not to forget that to adopt new values can be painful and create disturbances for the individual as well as for the whole community.

It has been my experience that to enable one to step out of his or her frame of reference and become aware of other possibilities of looking at reality, an exposure to different life situations is necessary. Let me illustrate this by an example.

Some years ago, I met a bishop who told me how he came to change his value system. He had been very optimistic about the way his country was dealing with marginalized people and he was convinced that there was no unfair treatment in dispensing justice. One day a police officer, not recognizing him as the bishop, literally kicked him out of his office, taking him for one of these "good for nothing" people. This "kick" opened his eyes to the true reality in his country and he started for the first time to see things from the underside of society, from the standpoint of the oppressed and poor. He concluded his story by saying: "The Bible became a totally different book for me. It was as if I was reading it for the first time."

> The shock we receive through such an exposure to the harsh realities of life and the resultant change of our perspective — we are now looking at the world through the eyes of the poor — is only of short duration and will not bring about a fundamental change in our value system if we do not feel the compelling need to be steeped in the spirit of poverty as it was lived by Jesus. In other words, we need to acquire a spirituality that supports our solidarity with the poor, a solidarity that is expressed in our standing together as Mary stood with John beneath the cross. And in this attitude we will experience a new source of strength and power. (David Fleming, *Pilgrim's Notebook*)

The required spirituality

The spirituality we need to develop, therefore, includes three basic emphases: a return to the historical Jesus, a lived experience with the poor and love expressed in terms of mercy and compassion.

The Historical Jesus

An appreciation of the historical Jesus remains absolutely necessary for us to experience concretely what it means to live the Kingdom by following him. Any authentic spirituality must orient itself towards Jesus and his central message. True conversion requires the same attitudes shown by Jesus towards the poor, the outcast, the rich, the powerful; in other words, the compassion and commitment with which he offered integral liberation.

This relevancy of Jesus' humanity becomes possible because of an increasing familiarity with the Gospel. One of the fascinating phenomena of our time is that the Bible is becoming the book of the simple people. They regard it as their book and are reading it, meditating on it alone or in groups. This gives them a new knowledge of the Jesus who walked this earth and who had to face all the hardships of life which they themselves experience day in and day out. And as the people read the Bible, they do so in order to practice what it says. They read with a profound respect, looking to what is written. They do not look to it to find their own ideas, but to hear the Word, to become inwardly silent so the Word can change them. This is reading the Bible with the reality as a point of departure, to keep in sight the faith of the community and to have a profound respect for the text, in other words, interpreting and understanding life and what God has to say today with the help of the Bible.

In the same way Mary, the Blessed Mother of Jesus, assumes a new role. She is primarily seen now as THE true disciple of Jesus and devotion to her offers the possibility for a new spirituality.

The life experience of the poor and needy

The concrete experience of life among the poor is the source from which a real concern for solidarity and justice emerges. A. Nolan in a talk on "The Services of the Poor and Spiritual Growth" distinguishes four stages in a commitment to the poor:

First, a COMPASSION that emerges out of exposure to suffering and misery which in turn motivates us to ACTION, be it relief work or the simplification of our own life-style.

The second stage is the discovery that poverty is a STRUCTURAL PROBLEM based on particular social and political situations, manufactured by humans, which create oppression and injustice. Our reaction is one of ANGER and INDIGNATION, directed in particular towards the rich and the politicians. To keep a balance between anger and compassion is a difficult task but it must be achieved. The reality of structural sin is realized and no individual conversion can possibly remove it. We come to realize that it is the system, which makes victims of us all, including the rich. It is this system that must be changed.

Some years ago I was invited to give some talks to the General Chapter of the Carmelites held in Manila. The topic was: Our preferential option for the poor. Prior to the Chapter itself the sixty men had been exposed for three weeks to marginalized groups all over the Philippines prior to the Chapter itself. This exposure turned out to have been traumatic for a number of them. It took quite a while before they were able to deal with their anger and indignation.

In the third stage we have to discover that the poor are PERFECTLY ABLE to save themselves and that they do not need us to save them. We come to see that we have to LEARN FROM THEM and that we do not have to teach them. We have to learn that it is the poor who are God's chosen instrument for transforming the world. This in turn becomes an experience of God acting in the midst of the struggle of the poor. The inherent danger here is one of romanticizing the poor.

The fourth stage means to move from DISILLUSIONMENT and DISAP-POINTMENT with the poor to true solidarity. One must realize that the poor are not automatically saints nor the rich sinners. The problem is structural. We are asked to explore our own backgrounds and from this vantage point to take up their cause, not our own. We discover the different roles we have to take up with them and not for them to overcome oppression and unjust structures. Once we come to see that the struggle of the poor is God's own cause, we will be able to overcome the disillusionment and disappointment with poor people which we all experience once we become involved.

Once upon a time there was a man who strayed from his own country into the world known as the Land of Fools. He soon saw a number of people flying in terror from a field where they had been trying to reap wheat. "There is a monster in that field," they told him. He looked and saw that the 'monster' was merely a watermelon.

He offered to kill the 'monster' for them. When he had cut the melon from its stalk, he took a slice and began to eat it. The people became even more terrified of him than they had been of the melon. They drove him away with pitchforks, crying, "He will kill us next, unless we get rid of him."

It so happened that shortly afterwards another man also strayed into the Land of Fools. But instead of offering to help the people with the 'monster', he agreed with them that it must be dangerous, and by tiptoeing away from it with them he gained their confidence. He spent a long time with them in their homes until he could teach them, little by little, the basic facts which would enable them not only to lose their fear of melons, but eventually to cultivate melons themselves. (H. Nouwen, *Compassion*)

Love expressed in Terms of Mercy and Compassion

If one gets through these stages and finds the way back to the Bible one will come to see God's way of doing things. The discovery of a compassionate God whom we want to follow is a great step in this spirituality. In the commitment to the poor a discovery is made: one comes to see what the driving force in Jesus' concern for us was, what moved him, what lay at the core of all his actions, namely MERCY and COMPASSION.

The Gospels use the word COMPASSION twelve times in connection with the suffering, distress and sorrow that affected the people whom Jesus encountered. His reaction to these predicaments is always compassion, meaning: he 'suffers with' the suffering person before he heals or takes the predicament away.

As we cannot understand the poor without Jesus, neither can we understand compassion independently of him. The challenge of the Gospel is most accurately expressed in the radical demand of Jesus: "You should be as compassionate as your Father in heaven is compassionate." And for us, as for Jesus, it is in the poor that we disco-ver God's compassion, his predilection and the mystery of his plan: that God has chosen them to be his agents for the salvation of the whole world. The experience of living with the poor leads to a deeper understanding of Jesus and the central message of the Kingdom which is, first of all, a message meant for the poor.

Option for the Poor: God's option not ours

It is not we or some theologians who invented this preferential option for the poor. It is God Himself who first made this preferential option for the poor. He decided to be on their side and chose them as his favorite agents to accomplish his intention with the world. Not the influential, not the powerful, not the learned but those who do not count. From such a perspective the whole of revelation looks different. Suddenly biblical texts assume a different meaning. The Exodus story is discovered as the key text which reveals to us the true nature of God. This story is central to the Bible and provides us with the first self-identification of God. Here the true essence of God is revealed in the sense that God clearly shows us who he will be in the history of humankind: the one who hears the cries of those living in oppression, and who is determined to do something about it. As the text expresses it:

> I have seen the miserable state of my people in Egypt. I have heard their cry
> to be free of their slave drivers. Yes, I am well aware of their suffering. I
> mean to deliver them out of the hand of their oppressors (Ex 3:7-9).

Our God is a God who sees, who hears, who is aware of the plight of the poor and who will not remain indifferent but who will come and do something about it, namely, he will deliver us. But here the trouble starts. God will not do this alone. He accomplishes it through his messengers. In order to fulfill his promise, God chose Moses, one of the oppressed, to be his agent of liberation: I send you to Pharaoh to bring the sons of Israel, my people, out of Egypt (Ex 3:10).

When Moses objects to this selection, the only reassurance he receives is, "I WILL BE WITH YOU." This phrase, "I will be with you," is the leitmotif throughout God's redeeming actions in history.

As Boff sees it, in the different liberation movements of our time one comes to realize the plan of God for humankind as a whole. He leads us from bondage into freedom once we commit ourselves to the poor. The poor are seen as a sacrament through which God reveals himself. Here we encounter God's own demand for solidarity, identification with and justice for the marginalized. The response to this call of God is to be understood as incarnating one's faith by clinging to the Lord present in the poor. The commitment of faith is seen as union with the poor Christ and the deep desire to live and to follow him alone. This is what Puebla meant by saying the "poor also evangelize the Church." Awareness of the poor makes it easier to find God, to understand the Gospel and to purify our prayer.

There is, however, one more twist in God's idea of the liberation of His people. His plan does not include, as some liberation theologians and many well-meaning Christians envision or hope for, a conversion of the oppressor and subsequently of the oppressive system through a group of people who consider themselves as God's chosen ones. God seems to be more realistic and more radical. He hardens the heart of Pharaoh and even allows him to solidify the oppressive structures while at the same time, He takes His chosen people out of the whole system.

According to Norbert F. Lohfink, God's option for the poor as described so vividly in the Exodus story has as its objective the creation of a "contrast society", because God leads his people OUT OF Egypt.

> ...Poor people are not just given some kind of aid; instead, the social system that produced their poverty is rejected in toto. They are removed from this system, and God creates out of them the miracle of a new society in contrast to all previous societies, a society in which there are no more poor. The beginning of a divine contrast-society: that is God's concrete and distinctive option for the poor in the meaning of the Exodus credo. (*Option for the Poor*)

Lohfink sees the basic communities as the embodiment of God's plans for a new society, as places of social transformation. They witness to "a new life in contrast to all that went before, a life built on the memory of Israel and of Jesus". Thus the "Church of the poor", as the liberation theologians call the basic communities, are the potential "new society which is emerging as church from among the liberated poor." To be a member of this new society presupposes that the person is a disciple of Jesus and tries to live as he lived. And this includes persecution as well as martyrdom, a reality that is experienced in those countries where people have made the option for the poor their life commitment.

> Where the gospel for Yahweh's poor truly prevails, the transformation of this world really happens. To everyone's astonishment, there comes into being the miracle of a society in which people can relate in a new way to material things and to one another and where, as a result, there is no poverty. But in the same measure as the members of this society experience the abolition of every kind of poverty, they also discover how the old society closes ranks against them and begins to persecute them. And the odd thing is that both of these experiences belong together and are intimately connected: that of the miracle of the abolition of poverty and at the same time that of being thrown back again into the poverty of persecution. (N. Lohfink p. 75)

If God wants to save this world through a group of people that provide a contrast to the mainstream of society then the criterion for belonging to this 'contrast society' is faithful discipleship to Jesus.

Jesus demonstrated in his own life God's preferential love for the poor. He was born in poverty (Lk 2:7); he had to work for his own bread (Mk 6:3), and he died naked (Jn 19:23-24). He cautioned the one who wanted to follow him wherever he would go by saying:

> Birds have nests and foxes have holes but the Son of Man has no place to lay down his head and rest (Mt 8:20).

Looking at Jesus as he walked this earth and feeling in oneself the call to follow him contains a risk. Where is it said in the Bible that those who would follow him would be insured against mishap? That their lives would be provided for? That they would belong to the affluent, the influential, the powerful?

The story of Zachaeus, told by Matthew, can be a pattern of conversion for those who want to follow him today. Zachaeus was rich but at the same time very small, so short in fact that he thought he had to climb a tree if he were to see Jesus surrounded by the poor and hear his message. Then Jesus called him down from the perch in the tree. The Lord invited him to join the poor so that he might understand the Good News from the only vantage point which could enable him to see and understand what Jesus is all about.

Option for the Poor: Change of values

It is not my intention to present to you the Liberation Theology in any length. This theology, however, has unearthed two basic elements which we cannot ignore. The first we may describe as the preferential option for the poor as the correct way to follow the Lord today.

The second is the insight that our status in society conditions not only our way of thinking and perceiving reality but also our way of reading the Bible and what we perceive as the Word of God for us today. I like to compare this with filters which we use when looking at reality. The issue is not the existence of filters but which filters do we use when reading the Word of God.

Theologians talk about the phenomenon of 'selective inattention' while looking at reality. We avert only to those facts and aspects of reality which in no way threaten our status and way of life. These facts and aspects are true, but our stress is excessive and so becomes disadvantageous to others. For it is here that our inborn tendency to have, to possess, to control and to dominate, makes itself felt. This effect is operative in so subtle and hidden a way that we do not realize it. The preferential option for the poor goes directly against such a tendency. A change of heart is needed, however, to see how we are tied to this inborn tendency and a real conversion is required to accept this option as one of the most essential aspects of following the Lord. Such an option for the poor does not come naturally; it is a gift and a consequence of true fellowship. We might only come to realize how essential such a commitment is in following the Lord after we have made it.

For such a conversion, a change of filters, a new way of looking and perceiving, a new way of experiencing reality are needed. We have to experience that the option for the poor makes us more alive, brings more joy and fulfillment into our lives. Only then will this way of following the Lord be accepted. For what is at stake are values. As I have mentioned before, one cannot teach values. They have to be discovered and to be experienced by the person himself or herself. Otherwise they will not be accepted and no behavioral change will happen. It all remains on the level of theory.

It is good to remember that the first disciples of Jesus had a hard time with regard to such a change. The change of filters did not come easily to them either. This can be seen in the utter amazement they showed when Jesus made it clear that no rich man could enter the Kingdom of heaven and that his way was to live in dependence on whatever the Father would give them (Mt 6:25-35; Mk 10: 23-

27). Their squabbling over the first places demonstrated that they had not yet grasped what the Kingdom was about (Mk 10:35-45). Even their last question is concerned with the hope of a splendid position in the Kingdom, "Lord, will you finally restore the Kingdom of Israel?" (Ac 1:6) Jesus' answer sounds like he had almost given up, that it was left to the Spirit to do a better job in helping them to understand. Seventeen times we hear Jesus complaining, "Can you not see; are your minds that dull; don't you understand, are you still without perception; how can you fail to understand?"

The need for healing

At times I feel it needs a miracle to cure our blindness and to open our ears to the cries of the poor, to take away our complacency, our indifference and fill our hearts with the compassion and love that Jesus himself revealed in his life. But the question is, do I really want the miracle to happen so that I may come to see and hear? Several times we read in Scripture that when people come to Jesus for healing he asks them first, "Do you want to be healed?" Or Jesus asks them, "What do you want me to do?" Jesus throws back to the person concerned the decision whether he really wants to be cured, to be able to see, to be able to hear, to be able to walk. Does the sick person really want to be healed considering the consequences that are contained in such a healing? If God heals me or you we might be led where we would rather not go (Jn 21). It could upset my whole way of life and my scale of values. Do I really want to see? At the same time, my personal conversion might begin when I, instead of being so sure about what the poor should do to better their lives, like Jesus, ask them, "What do you want me to do for you?"

Our ways and God's ways of acting

The Bible could be described as the book that contains God's design for the whole of creation along with the power to realize this design: the transformation of the whole of creation into the New Heaven and the New Earth. But how does he accomplish this? What is his plan of action, what means does he use?

Anyone who reads the Bible carefully will sooner or later come to understand: God's ways are not our ways. Humanly speaking God seems to be particularly weak on logic. His dealing with us does not go through his intellect but through his heart. His ways of accomplishing his purpose are strange and most of the time they are exactly the opposite of how human reasoning would proceed. The trouble is that we often fail to grasp this, and plan all our activities and endeavors along the lines of human reasoning. The basic rules of the Kingdom are not success and competition but faithfulness and compassion. These are virtues with which you could never run a human business. God's messengers and agents are described in the Bible in these words:

> God purposely chose what the world considers nonsense in order to put wise men to shame, and what the world considers weak in order to put powerful men to shame. He chose what the world looks down on, and despises, and thinks is nothing, in order to destroy what the world thinks is important (1 Co 1:27).

To accept such a view, I have to change a lot of filters and let my reasoning be silenced. This is apparently crazy; it goes against all the rules and logic of this world. And yet this is the conversion we are challenged to go through today. That is what the option for the poor ultimately means. A text like the above suddenly receives a new meaning. By identifying the "nonsense and the weak" in this passage with the powerless and exploited of the present world, the role of the poor in the history of salvation is discovered anew. The problem with us, however, is that we never really identified ourselves with the proud, but instinctively regarded ourselves as the ones God had chosen in order to put "the wise of this world" to shame.

The question often heard today is: how can we make God's voice heard again in a secularized world which seemingly can do without him? How can we proclaim him in a world of massive injustice and oppression? Where can we ourselves hear his voice clearly and discover his presence in the world today?

Anyone who has some pastoral experience knows that God never solves problems for us: He only points out a direction. The signs of the time indicate the direction: a commitment to the poor. What will we gain through such a commitment? First, we will again experience the liberating power of the message of Jesus. We will be set free: freed from the belief that only the possession of things will guarantee a true unfolding of our lives; freed from the temptation to settle for a comfortable life and thus compromise the Gospel.

Years ago I worked for some months with a group of volunteers in Calcutta related to Mother Teresa's work. One night we could not go back to our home and had to sleep wherever there was a place left on the sidewalk. I was deeply worried and woke up every five minutes, afraid something might happen. While praying, it occurred to me that for the first time in my life I was put into a situation for the Gospel's sake in which Jesus and his disciples often found themselves. The word of Jesus, addressed to the one who wanted to follow him wherever he would go, came to my mind, "Foxes have holes and birds have nests but the Son of Man has no place to rest." It filled me with an immense joy and peace lifting all worry and anxiety. At least that one time I lived as Jesus lived. I will never forget that night.

The survival and revitalization of religious congregations seem to depend on whether they recognize the signs of the times and have the humility to rethink their commitment to the Lord in the light of how God reveals his redeeming power today in the poor. The option for the poor is not a matter of choice for us, but a matter of survival. It could well be the greatest challenge we are facing today as religious congregations and as Church.

Conclusion

If we could come in our time to a new awareness of what true Gospel values are and if we would start rethinking our whole commitment to Christ in the light of this discovery, I think our generation would have done its share. Nothing is achieved by issuing big statements concerning the option for the poor if we cannot make people change their value systems. And they will not change their value system if we cannot make them aware of new and different ways of looking at the Gospel. But that requires an insight which must be gained by people themselves. Liberation theologians have always insisted that nobody will understand or come to see what they are talking about without having a prior commitment to the liberation of the poor. It all depends, therefore, on whether or not I can lead people in the direction that would enable them to make such a commitment. Otherwise all our beautiful sounding statements concerning the preferential option for the poor will remain empty and shallow. They will never change the commitment or outlook of religious congregations. The answer we give to this challenge today will determine if our congregations have a future.

Questions for Reflection:

1. What is my personal reaction to the call to a 'preferential option for the poor?'

2. How do I manifest my belonging to a 'contrast society' that God has charged with the task of salvation for the world?

3.How willing am I to examine the possibility of just how much my personal style of life, the style of life in my community, is sustained by structures that are detrimental or even oppressive for others?

4.What 'filters' prevent me from seeing the world and God's plans for our salvation in the way he wants them to be seen?

5.What steps have I taken from 'talking about the poor' to 'talking with the poor', which indicates that my preferential option is beginning to take concrete shapes?

Stroy for Reflection:

FORGETTING TO WHOM THINGS BELONG

A very proper lady went to a tea shop. She sat at a table for two, ordered a pot of tea, and prepared to eat some cookies which she had in her purse. Because the tea shop was crowded, a man took the other chair and also ordered tea. As it happened, he was a Jamaican black, though that is not essential to the story. The woman was prepared for a leisurely time, so she began to read her paper. As she did so, she took a cookie from the package. As she read, she noticed that the man across also took a cookie from the package. This upset her greatly, but she ignored it and kept reading. After a while she took another cookie. And so did he. This unnerved her and she glared at the man. While she glared, he reached for the fifth and last cookie, smiled and offered her half of it. She was indignant. She paid her money and left in a great hurry, enraged at such a presumptuous man. She hurried to her bus stop just outside. She opened her purse to get a coin for her bus ticket. And then she saw, much to her distress, that in her purse was her package of cookies unopened. (W. Brueggemann, *To Act Justly, Love Tenderly, Walk Humbly*)

Brueggemann draws the following conclusion:

The lady is not different from all of us. Sometimes we possess things so long that do not really belong to us that we come to think they are ours. Sometimes by the mercy of God, we have occasion to see to whom these things in fact belong. And when we see that, we have some little chance of being rescued from our misreading of reality. Justice concerns precisely a right reading of social reality, of social power, and of social goods.

FOLLOWING THE CELIBATE JESUS: CELIBACY FOR LIVING, NOT FOR KEEPING

Introduction

Much has been said and written about "the crisis of celibate life." Indeed, in some circles there's a hostile attitude towards celibacy. Maybe it's not out in the open, but it's there on the socio-cultural level, that is, in the milieu in which we live. But celibacy as such does not exist, celibates exist and most probably will go on existing.

There are in the world more than one million religious and priests who have chosen the celibate state of life. It would be presumptuous to state categorically that these one million people are all unhappy with their celibate life in spite of the many who have left the life over the years. A crisis doesn't necessarily mean an end. It forces us to go back to roots. And so the underlying question we need to ask is: did Jesus, who required poverty and obedience from everyone who wanted to follow him, envision a form of discipleship that demanded a celibate life, i.e., so radical a dedication to him that the disciple is asked to forego marriage and to give himself/herself totally to him and his cause, the Kingdom of God?

The biblical roots of celibacy

There are three basic issues we need to reflect on to respond to this question: first, what Scripture says about such a way of life; second, whether Jesus was a celibate; and, third, whether he invited others to embrace this state.

The Bible and celibacy

Generally it can be said that although the celibate state at the time of Jesus was known among marginal communities and apocalyptic figures, the mainstream of theological thinking was suspicious of it and rejected it as unbiblical. A rabbinical saying indicates that "to allow one's twentieth birthday to pass without one's having married, is to break a command and draw down on oneself the anger of God."

The Genesis command to "increase and multiply" was seen as an absolute divine mandate. The Talmud reflects the rabbinic doctrine that refusal to marry was a sin: "One who does not marry is like a person who sheds blood — he refuses to transmit the life within him."

Celibacy was opposed to the feeling and sentiment of Jesus' time because it was held that, through marriage, a person could see the days of the Messiah, i.e., that through living on in his or her children he or she could participate in their life in the days of the coming age. To be childless was seen as a curse, a punishment from God since it would exclude the person from the future Messianic age. This was the reason why the brother of a man who died without children had to take his sister-in-law and have children with her so that his dead brother would have part in the messianic age through the children of his brother from his wife (Mt 22:23-27).

Was Jesus himself celibate?

The New Testament does not specifically state that Jesus was a celibate, but that he lived as a celibate during his public ministry cannot be doubted. The claim made by some exegetes that Jesus was indeed married before he started his preaching is an assumption based on the general custom that every male Jew would get married at the age of eighteen. But if we assume that Jesus was in contact with the movement of John the Baptist, his being a celibate becomes probable.

There are two texts in the New Testament which refer directly to the question of celibacy: Mt 19:10-12 and 1 Co 7:25-35.

There are different reasons why men cannot marry: some because they were born that way; others, because men made them that way; and others do not marry because of the Kingdom of Heaven. Let him who can do it accept this teaching (Mt 19:10-12).

These words seem to be a justification by Jesus of his own celibacy. It shocked and surprised the people of his times. They had called him a glutton, a drunkard, a friend of tax collectors. So they seemed to have found another insult for him: eunuch, a term that was extremely offensive among Jews, and even more among Greeks. Jesus would hardly have used the offensive term in a context of positive praise unless it had been hurled at him in the midst of a controversy. In answer to this insult Jesus gives his reply.

The text is saying that some men are impotent by nature, some are made that way, and there are those who are celibate because the imminent coming of the Kingdom of God has turned their attention and interest elsewhere. Jesus declares that he is neither impotent nor a eunuch, but that he has a much more valid reason to remain unmarried — for the sake of the Kingdom. It is the arrival of the Kingdom, i.e., God's unconditional love for us — which Jesus experienced so intensely in himself that he felt utterly overwhelmed by it, and felt impelled to direct all his human capacity for loving to the Father.

Did Jesus reccommend this way of life to others?

Of the over forty commentaries I have consulted on this passage, a slight majority of commentators would admit that this text of Matthew does refer to Jesus' own state of celibacy and that it does contain an invitation to others to follow him in that way of life. Others see the text in connection with divorce. It is the overpowering presence of the Kingdom that can give the person the strength to remain unmarried if his first marriage breaks down. But if the passage refers to celibacy, it would also be the overpowering presence of the Kingdom that would give the person the strength to remain unmarried.

In case one feels called to the unmarried state this is not something one can embrace of one's own choosing. It is to be seen as a vocation from God. "Not everyone can understand this word, only those to whom it is granted by God." The Greek "DIA" indicates the reason for such a choice — the imminent Kingdom. Therefore, celibacy freely chosen becomes a sign of the Kingdom present. The reality of the Kingdom is experienced by some people as so overpoweringly present that they are seized, grasped and swept away by it. They are so taken up by this reality that they feel that there is no room left for dedicating oneself to another person in marriage.

St. Paul's text on celibacy 1 Cor 7:25-35, is definitely eschatological, referring to the presence of the Kingdom now. For him, celibacy is a gift from God belonging to the end-time. One of the fundamental structures of the present world is marriage. By not marrying, one gives clear witness to the fact that the end-time has come. Celibacy makes the person free to pursue fully the "things of the Lord" which are the "new order", the "new creation", the "Kingdom of God". For Paul, celibacy is a personal orientation to the Lord, a freedom for focusing on him alone, a freedom for undistracted friendship with the Lord. Celibacy makes him free for the Lord and his mission.

The contemplative and apostolic dimension of celibacy?

Every vow is a gift from the Lord to follow him in this way of life. Something we do not choose on our own. It is a call to discipleship. It follows the pattern of any call: it is a gift (*I chose you*); to become a disciple (*to be with me*); and to be an apostle (*to be sent out*). Every vow, besides being a gift from the Lord, therefore, contains two dimensions which we may call the contemplative (*being with the Lord*) and the apostolic (*being sent*). We might also call the first the 'spirituality' of the vow and second the 'actual living out' of the vow, or the missionary aspect.

THE CONTEMPLATIVE DIMENSION OF CELIBACY: "being with the Lord"

Celibacy is an invitation to follow one aspect of the life- style of Jesus. Celibacy is a personal gift from God that orientates my whole being towards the Father of Jesus Christ, so that I am seized and taken up by the love of God in Jesus. As a result, I cannot but give myself to him freely and totally. This is possible, from the viewpoint of human nature, since the ultimate aim and goal of all persons is union and communion with God. Every human being on the face of the earth has an existential thirst for God. Celibacy, then, can be seen as the ultimate expression of this desire to love God, now, to the full capacity of the human heart. Yet we always have to remember, it is not of a free choosing, it is and remains a love-gift from God and therefore it can never be fully explained.

Celibacy is a very complex reality. More exactly, it is a **MYSTERY** whose richness calls more for contemplation and appreciation than for analysis or explanation. The choice of lifelong celibacy bears upon the most intimate core of human existence. It is a choice that matures in the context of a religious experience of more than ordinary intensity, and is not always completely separable from the more global experience of religious life. (Sandra M.Schneiders *New Wineskins*)

The mystical dimension of celibacy

The difficulty (if not impossibility) of celibacy lies exactly in this last part of the sentence - that I intend to live presently in a state of life which belongs, as a promise, to the future. I feel so taken up by this future life, which breaks into my life at this time, that I want to live it now, in the present condition of this world. If I do this, my life becomes a witness to the belief that God's ultimate redeeming love is not just something in the future, but a reality that is already present in this world.

God's love is present in some people in such a tangible and experiential way they feel themselves seized by it to the point that it demands their total capacity to love. Indeed, this love is so strong that those who experience it are able to forego marriage and family life for the sake of the overpowering reality that this love includes. But since this love of God is not an abstraction but a very concrete reality, namely, Jesus Christ, celibacy, as St. Paul saw it, becomes a personal orientation to the Lord and brings with it a freedom to focus on him alone. The real depth of celibacy exists, therefore, in an exclusive dedication to the Lord, which makes a similar focusing on anyone else impossible.

Ignace Lepp, a French priest-psychologist, once said that he would not advise celibacy to anyone but a mystic. What he actually meant was that he would not advise celibacy to anyone unwilling to grow in a deep prayer communion with the Lord. One who cannot move into this depth of love with the Lord should enter or even stay in that way of life which by its nature demands such depth.

According to H. Nouwen, celibacy is a life-style in which we try to witness to the **priority of God in all relationships.** By manifesting this in every facet of our lives we lead others to question some of their basic assumptions and actions. For the celibate person **contemplative prayer** is an essential element of his life, because it brings about a gradual emptying that God alone wants to fill.

Contemplative prayer is not a way of being busy with God instead of with people, but it is an attitude in which we recognize God's ultimate priority by **being useless in his presence,** by standing in front of him without anything to show, to prove or to argue, and by allowing him to enter into our emptiness...both, contemplative prayer and celibacy are expressions of being vacant for God. Contemplative prayer as **standing naked, power-less, and vulnerable before God,** therefore, is one of the most important expressions of the celibate life-style. (H. J. Nouwen, *Clowning in Rome*)

True contemplative prayer, in which the celibate develops a warm, affectionate, and intimate prayer life leads us to an experience of the gentle, caring love of God.

> In this contemplative prayer we **become really free**, we sense that we are accepted, that we belong, that we are not totally alone but that we live in the embrace of him whose fatherhood includes motherly, brotherly, and sisterly love. Once **we really know him in prayer** then we can live in this world without a need to cling to anyone for self-affirmation, and then we can let the abundance of God's love be the source of all our ministry. (*Clowning in Rome*)

The eschatological dimension of celibacy

Celibacy is only livable when there is a constant openness to and expectation of the final coming of the Lord. It is an existence based on hope. It is the constant attempt to live totally facing the future. As a life in the Church and for the Church, it reminds the people of God not to forget that aspect of their Christian existence that is 'preliminary' before the Lord comes again. Celibates are people on the road towards a future fulfillment. The celibate life asks the disciple to be in constant readiness — to stay awake and attentive to meet the Lord when he comes. Celibates are not unlike the ten wise virgins in the parable. In this sense celibates are utopian people. They are of this world, but constantly pointing to that coming reality from which the present world is to receive its meaning and according to which it must be reshaped.

> Christian celibacy is an evangelical mystery, a charism inaugurated in the Church by Jesus himself. As long as our understanding of the "reign of God" is incomplete, so will be our understanding of consecrated celibacy chosen "because" of that reign. We do not fully understand what Jesus meant by the reign of God. But as the community of the disciples journeys through history we see different meanings in this intensive symbol of the fullness of salvation. (Sandra M.Schneiders, *ibid.*)

The sexual dimension of celibacy

Celibates have to live this "utopian" life in the context of this world. That means, concretely, that they have to reckon with human sexuality and the human need for affection and love.

a.Celibates must not overlook the obvious fact that they are distinctively male or female in every cell of their bodies. Yes, celibacy must reckon with human sexuality. Genuine celibacy does involve, of course, a renunciation, but only of erotic activity and of conjugal and family life, as spiritual writers call it. But to renounce being virile and paternal or feminine and maternal would be an unacceptable and damaging mutilation. There is a great value and even a necessity for every celibate to care for a healthy relationship with others, particularly with the complementary sex, with the precise understanding, however, that such relationships are continent and non-erotic.

b. We should not overlook the fact that a natural explanation for celibacy is not possible. Therefore, the celibate will always be a kind of stranger, and will know loneliness. This makes it all the more necessary for celibates to form true communities with one another. They need each other's affirmation that this way of life is as meaningful today as it has been through the past twenty centuries of Christian life. They need friendship and mutual support in order to live such a way of life today.

c. Some years ago I read a passage in H. Nouwen's book, *intimacy*, which proved helpful to me in counselling   priests and religious. He stated that to be able to live a healthy life in this world, which judges me and asks me to play a role according to my identity as male or female, two things are necessary:

First, I must have my own inner privacy where I can be myself and find new strength to face the challenging world.

Second, I must establish a hierarchy of relationships within this same world. In the inner circle of my life I find one or two persons who are closest to me. Around this circle of intimacy I find the circle of friends and family. Then, in a somewhat larger circle, I locate relatives and acquaintances, and, even further away, my associates in business and work. In the final circle, there is everyone else. Nouwen concludes, "A vowed person without a spiritual life and a good friend is like sounding brass or tinkling cymbal."

The apostolic dimension of celibacy

The Rule of Taize introduces its chapter on celibacy with these words:

> While celibacy brings greater opportunities to concern oneself with the things of the Lord, it is acceptable only in order to give oneself more fully to one's neighbor with the love of Christ.

The vow of celibacy should enable me to love more, not less. Jesus was a celibate but that did not keep him aloof from people. He was a man who loved people with all the warmth of human love. He loved children, and revealed a remarkable openness to women, something not common for a rabbi (Mk 10:13-16; Mt 18:1-24). He had friends, people he loved more than others and whom he loved deeply: Lazarus, Martha and Mary (Jn 11:5; 35) and there was John, the Beloved Disciple, for whom he had a special affection (Jn 13:23-25; 21:20).

With this vow I offer to the Lord my natural capacity to love and I make it available to him to be a carrier of his saving love for the world. The celibate life becomes an incarnation and a bearer of God's saving love to others. As God's love came to us in Christ the Man, so it comes to others through my dedicated life. Celibacy becomes apostolic celibacy. It should enable me to love more compassionately, to be more gentle, more understanding, more kind. In short, more Christ-like.

> Two Buddhist monks were out walking when they came to a large sheet of water which stretched across their path. A young girl was also standing there, not knowing how to cross to the other side. One of the monks picked her up in his arms and carried her across. The monks then continued their walk. Half an hour later, the second monk said to the first, "Why did you do that? You know, that as monks we are not even permitted to look at a woman or touch her, let alone pick her up in our arms." "Ah, my brother," said the first monk, "the difference between you and me is that I left the girl back by the pool of water."° (Indian legend, Paul J. Wharton)

To "keep" my celibacy is not enough. I must live it. To abstain from erotic activity and from conjugal and family life does not yet mean I live a life of celibate love. There are scores of substitutes for and aberrations of celibacy, whereby one might keep the vow, but not really live it at all. How often do we hear the complaints of married women who tell us, "I am not my husband's wife. His wife is his hobby, his car, his football, his golf, his dog, his parrot, his horses, etc." Similar things could be said about celibates. Love of God and others is not what is central in their lives, but rather their hobby, be it golf, photography, a stamp collection, or some animal, not to mention the big problems like alcohol, homosexuality, etc. I knew a cardinal who had a huge doll collection he spent hours with. There is nothing against having a hobby (it may keep you sane), but I need to make sure it does not become my substitute for celibate love.

There are three possibilities I can live this great gift from God by being fully committed to the vow. I can become a bachelor or a spinster, "keeping" celibacy perfectly but in no way living it in true loving service for others; or I can be a hypocrite, pretending that I live celibacy but in reality not doing so.

A fulfilled celibate life will only be possible for those who really see celibacy as a gift from God. This gift they joyfully accept as a charism to be lived for the good of one's brothers and sisters by witnessing to them the all-pervasive presence of the Kingdom. The only reason for celibacy is the Kingdom present and not as St. Thomas held that it is a state of abstinence and therefore leads to greater perfection.

The vow of celibacy should make us more loving, more affectionate and more joyful. Celibacy is not for keeping but for living. It might sound strange, but we all know how easily we can exclude our own brothers and sisters in our religious community from our love. We all know how merciless in judgement and uncompassionate we can be towards them!

In order to see whether we are really living celibate love or not, we ought to reflect on these questions:

1.Do I really care for the others in community with a compassionate love, i.e., bearing others' burdens, being present to others and not just being a superficial acquaintance?

2.Am I a person who acknowledges readily and gladly the good things that others do? Am I able to say a word of appreciation and really mean it? Or do I never get over a kind of indifference, because I feel no one appreciates me, or jealousy when I see others doing something I could never do as well as they?

3.Am I generous with others or do I let my brothers and sisters 'pay' for what I do for them. Hospitality was the most treasured virtue in the early Church. Am I a hospitable person, who welcomes strangers into my home without caring how much it costs?

4.Am I a thankful person? In such persons there is an alertness to the goodness existing all around them. Can I see God's goodness in the little things around me? In what people do for me? Or do I take everything for granted? What is more enjoyable than a grateful and thankful person? These are people "with a heart".

5.All human beings cry for affirmation, acceptance and love. Am I an affirming person? Am I a person who sees loneliness, depression and even despair in other people and moves spontaneously to alleviate these sufferings with compassionate love? C.B. Baars who has written a lot of books on psychology and religious life, once remarked, "In our opinion, the reason why such alarming numbers of ordained priests and professed religious have left their state of life in recent decades must be sought more in the area of non-affirmation than in repressed sexual needs."

6.Concerning our pastoral activities, we could say that

Celibacy as an evangelical and apostolic virtue is the expression of an insatiable longing for the day of the Lord. It impels us towards solidarity with those unmarried people whose celibacy (that is to say, loneliness; that is to say, not having anyone) is not a virtue but their social destiny, and towards those who are shut up in lack of expectation and in resignation. (Johannes Metz, *Followers of Christ*)

To this group belong the old people in our society who have no one to love them or to pull them out of their desperate loneliness and isolation. There are also those who, as a result of broken marriages, or of families that have come apart, have been driven into a helpless isolation that lacks all promise. To live celibacy means to have an eye and a heart for all these people.

I used to give this advice to seminarians as well as to priests and religious in middle age who asked similar questions, who had doubts as to whether they could ever be faithful to celibacy. To live celibacy,

1. You must have a healthy mistrust of your own moral capacity. We are male or female and we will remain so as long as we live. One has to know one's commitment but also the longings of one's heart.

2. Make your resolve to commit yourself totally, radically to Christ and his way of life into a constant prayer for perseverance. Openness to the Kingdom and its power in prayer, and a true spiritual life, are the pillars of our commitment in this radical celibate way of following the Lord.

3. Live your vow humanly, but LIVE it and don't just keep it. Celibacy is for living. If you truly care for people and want to communicate God's love to them, you have to remember that God's love wants to reach them through your human capacity to love.

And I would go on to add: You should not stop committing yourself again and again to this way of life in spite of occasional failures.

The celibate is like the clown in the circus who, between the scary acts of the trapeze artists and lion tamers, fumbles and falls, reminding us that all human activities are ultimately not so important as the virtuosi make us believe. Celibates live out the holy emptiness in their lives by not trying to build for themselves a house or a fortune, by not trying to wield as much influence as possible, and by not filling their lives with events, people, or creations for which they will be remembered. They hope that by their empty lives God will be recognized as the source of all human thoughts and actions. (*Clowning in Rome*)

Questions for Reflection

1. Do I really desire to live a spiritual life, i.e., spend time on my relationship with the Lord in order to grow in love for him?

2. How do I live my celibacy? Do I experience it as an energy, a life-giving force? Am I a loving and caring person or am I just a bachelor or a spinster? Do I compensate for my celibate life in inappropriate ways?

3. Do I really have a genuine love and concern for those with whom I live?

4. Am I concerned that our houses are places where members of my own congregation and visitors are welcomed and feel at home?

5. In dealing with people do I radiate God's love to them?

Story for Reflection:

SOLITUDE

A carpenter and his apprentice were walking together through a large forest. And when they came across a tall, huge, gnarled, old, beautiful oak tree, the carpenter asked his apprentice, "Do you know why this tree is so tall, so huge, so gnarled, so old and beautiful?" The apprentice looked at his master and said, "No - why?" "Well, "the carpenter said, "because it is useless. If it had been useful, it would have been cut long ago and made into tables and chairs, but because it is useless it could grow so tall and so beautiful that you can sit in its shade and relax."° (Henri Nouwen, *Out of Solitude*)

Henri Nouwen continues:

In solitude we can grow old freely without being preoccupied with our usefulness and we can offer a service which we had not planned on...

Do you dare to be useless to become 'beautiful for the Lord and a gift to his people'?

PRAYER FOR THE GIFT OF CHASTITY

Lord Jesus, I ask you humbly for new grace, for a great increase in the charism of consecrated chastity. In virtue of your own risen and glorified sexuality, heal me in my own sexuality. Make the rough ways smooth and the crooked ways straight.

Heal me in the whole area of my affectivity, of my capacity to love and to receive love. Teach me your ways, and make me grow in my capacity to love you and to love others, to receive your love and to receive the love of others.

In every Eucharist, consecrate my whole self to you by your body, broken on the cross for me and risen for my salvation. Heal me by your five wounds that you still carry for me, and make me whole. Give me, Lord, your Holy Spirit, and pour out in me your gift of consecrated chastity.

Amen.

(R. Faricy)

FOLLOWING THE OBEDIENT JESUS: OBEDIENCE IN THE SETTING OF GROUP CHARISM

Introduction

We make the vow of obedience in order "to follow the Lord more freely and to imitate him more exactly as he presents himself in the Gospels" (P.C.2). It is the lifestyle of Jesus that inspires us to commit ourselves to this vow. We want to grow deeper into him and carry on his mission more faithfully. This must remain the ultimate reason why we submit to obedience in religious life.

The question that we have to ask again here is simple: What role did obedience play in the life of Jesus and what did he expect from those who would follow him? A close look into the life of Jesus shows that his whole life was ruled by the will of the Father. He regarded that will as his food.

My food it is to do the will of him who sent me (Jn 4:34).

His Father meant everything to Jesus. From him he drew his life. To please him was his only desire and aspiration. Yet Jesus had to struggle against the will of the Father all his life. There are a number of passages which clearly indicate this struggle:

He always had the very nature of God...Of his own free will he gave it all up...He became like man.. He walked the path of obedience to death (Ph 2:6-8).

In his life on earth Jesus made his prayers and requests with loud cries and tears to God, who could save him from death. Because he was humble and devoted, God heard him. But even though he was God's son he learned to be obedient by means of suffering (Heb 5:7-8).

Jesus did not get his will in his life on earth. Only with intense prayer and great agony was he able to do what the Father wanted him to do. The Father's will was his delight but it was also his agony when he had to go to the cross. What did Jesus expect from those who wanted to follow in his life-style?

The contemplative aspect of the vow of obedience: "to be with him"

1. *The imitation of Jesus' lifestyle*

To follow the Lord involves a process of gradually acquiring the attitudes and imitating the behavior of Jesus himself. The vow of obedience can only be understood by one who walks in the footsteps of the Lord. It is he I want to imitate. There will be situations in my life, as there were in the life of Jesus, when the will of God might be hard or impossible to fulfill according to human standards. There may be situations in which I might be "led where I would rather not go" (Jn 21:18). Without a deep devotion to Christ and a Christ-like mind, there is no chance that I will be able to go that way. Obedience is a gift from God that should lead me into closer fellowship with Christ, and, deeper into his mission. After all, we cannot and should not forget that we have entered into fellowship with a crucified Master, who at times will ask for the kind of obedience that was part of his own life.

2. *God's will as mediated through others*

The vow of obedience rests on the firm belief that God does not communicate his will to me directly, but through other persons. The vow asks for the virtue of humility, which knows well that we are in constant danger of mistaking our own will for God's will. Without such a belief, it is impossible to see a great value in the vow of obedience. Certainly, without such faith I will find it difficult to discover the will of God for me and my ministry. We cannot look at this vow in functional terms only. It presupposes the above interior attitudes, since the vows are not a commitment to a cause, noble as it may be, but to a living person — Jesus Christ.

The apostolic dimension of the vow of obedience: "to be sent out"

Religious life is a charism and, therefore, a gift of the Holy Spirit to the individual person so that he/she may fulfill a function in the Church for the well-being of the Church. Therefore, the vow of obedience has an apostolic dimension, i.e., it is meant to engage the person called to participate more actively in the mission of Christ in and for the Church. This leads us to the functional aspect of this vow.

1. Christian calling as a charism

According to St. Paul and to Scripture in general, any call by Yahweh or the Holy Spirit must be understood in terms of a charism. That means the call is always given to someone to fulfill a function within the community, for the benefit or the well-being of others or the entire group. One could also say that a charism is always a participation in the mission of Christ, a mission that constantly aims at the salvation of the whole of creation.

This is the way Paul describes charism in Rm 12 and 1 Co 12. For him a charism is the outward manifestation of the 'charis' given to someone when Christ calls the person into union and communion with him. This means that a Christian is given a charism or charisms which he/she is called to exercise for the well-being of the community. For example, if one has the gift of "faith" or "prayer" or "teaching" or "serving", these are gifts not given to the person for his or her benefit. The primary obligation of anyone with a charism is to exercise this gift in order that the whole body might stay healthy and well. In fact, one's very being is a "gift", a grace, a means by which salvation is mediated to others.

The exercise of the different charisms creates and keeps alive the entity which we call Church. It is correct to say that the individual member in the Christian community is kept alive and healthy in his or her commitment to the Lord through the exercise of the charisms of the members of the community. Paul's comparison of the Church with the living organism of the body is well known. The individual member lives and stays alive only as part of the whole; the entire body lives and stays alive only as long as the individual members fulfill their special function for the well-being of the whole. One wonders why we have so often forgotten this fundamental aspect of our vocation and have become so individualistic in our thinking.

The importance of 'a few people' was impressed on me by a missionary in Papua New Guinea.

He worked in the Highlands, in a very remote place. I visited him one day and was really startled to see how difficult life in his station was. Everyday there was fighting among the tribes which were supposed to be Christians. So I asked him, "How can you stand all this? It seems that nothing of your preaching reaches these people, why do you hold out?" His answer was simple. He said, "Here in my parish there are maybe four or five members whom I know have really understood the message of the Gospel better than I ever did. I have seen these people, I have seen them pray, I have seen them act. They are the ones that carry the faith, and their seeds will bear fruit in due season, I know that. I cannot leave these people alone, they are the hope of this parish."

My personal salvation depends on the activation of the charisms of the other members of the Church, just as their salvation is related to how I exercise or live out my particular charism. Salvation is, therefore, intrinsically bound up with community. The individual finds salvation not as an isolated individual, but insofar as he or she is a member of the Christian community. Our entire view of humankind and the world will change once we make this "communitarian view" of salvation a basis for our Christian spirituality. God's saving love is first of all directed towards the whole human race. His intense interest in and love for me and each human being is based on the fact that I am a member of this human community.

I always like to say, humorously, that when you go to present yourself to the Lord in prayer, always remember that God looks at you with only one eye. With the other eye he looks at the whole world which you present at that moment. We can never, in this sense, stand alone before God. We will always bring along every human being that lives and ever lived. Individual salvation without relation to the whole community is not possible.

The Woman and the Onion

Once upon a time there lived an old woman who was mean, very mean indeed. One day she died. Throughout her life she had never done a single good deed. Thus the angels came, picked her up and threw her into the fiery sea. Her guardian angel was standing by trying to think of a single good deed she had done in order to inform God about it. Suddenly he remembered one and mentioned it to God, "A long time ago she pulled an onion out of her vegetable patch and gave it to a poor beggar woman."

To this God replied, "Take that very same onion and hold it out to her in the fiery sea so that she can grasp it and pull herself up with the help of the onion. And if in this way you can pull her out of the sea, she may enter paradise. If, however, the onion breaks off she shall remain right there where she is."

The angel went on his way and held out the onion for her. He encouraged her to hold on to it so that he could pull her out. She grasped it tightly and he - ever so gently - began to pull. She was almost out of the fiery sea when the other sinners realized what was happening. They clung to her as their last means to escape the torments of the fire. But the old woman got very angry. She became so furious at the thought that they would be pulled out together with her that she kicked them back with her feet shouting, "This is MY onion and not yours! It is supposed to pull me out alone!

The very moment she said this, the onion split into two and the old woman fell back into the fiery sea and is still burning there up to this day. The angel cried and walked away. (F.M. Dostojewski)

If I can accept this "holistic view" of salvation my whole outlook on my vow of obedience and religious life will change accordingly.

2. Religious life as a charism

If every call is for the benefit of the whole, then religious life itself has to be seen as a charism, i.e., a gift to be exercised for the well-being of the Church and the redemption of the world. One can speak of a "group charism". Religious life should be regarded as such. This means that the whole group is called to exercise a charism for the benefit of the entire Church and its mission.

The Holy Spirit calls one person to take up a particular function in the Church for the benefit of the whole and, in turn, to gather a group of men or women around him or her to undertake this task in common. In such a case, the charism is seen as a collective gift. One could also explain it this way: the Spirit, who inspires the founder or foundress to form a new group in the Church, gives to other persons a kind of sensitivity so that they feel drawn to join this group. The whole group becomes responsible in this way for the group charism.

The spirituality of a particular congregation normally illuminates one aspect of the Gospel so that a better understanding of that aspect may be had. The group is then seen as a gift of the Holy Spirit which enables all in the group to live the initial insight of the founder or foundress. These insights are insights into the life of Christ and his mission. Each institute therefore is a perpetual renewal of the work of Christ in the Church and the world.

I would like to say something about the vow of obedience in its apostolic dimension, taking into account the view of religious life as a "group charism".

a. If religious life is a group charism the Holy Spirit wants to be exercised in the Church, then the individual religious who joins the group must assume personal responsibility for this charism. This he or she does in union with the entire congregation in a twofold way:

FIRSTLY, with the rest of the community I am responsible for constantly asking how the charism is to be **UNDERSTOOD** in the setting of our time, ever faithful to the original inspiration of the founder or foundress.

SECONDLY, I am, together with the community, responsible for how this charism is **EXERCISED** in the Church of today. I cannot leave it up to a few persons in the congregation to worry about it.

If I embrace the group charism, I will have to agree that it is going to determine, to a considerable extent, my personal life and life-style, i.e., my life as a religious is going to be concretized according to the charism of the congregation I join. In short, I put myself at the service of this charism and this charism in turn is going to determine my whole life.

This is very important for each religious to understand. If I join a missionary congregation, my religious life, i.e., the way I live the vows, will be determined by a missionary aspect and not vice-versa. This can have far-reaching consequences for me. It implies, for example, my willingness to leave or accept tasks and obligations once the group as a whole realizes that the charism of the congregation demands a shift in my apostolate.

> Evangelical obedience is not a simple response to a norm, a commandment or an order, that is, to a purely juridical and disciplinary reality, but, rather, **an habitual attitude of communion with a group and its leaders in faith and in love.** It should be noted that obedience, not only as communion in faith but also as communion in charity, has an essential relation with God and his salvific will. (John M. Lozano, *Life as Parable*)

I once asked the head of a major religious superiors' association what she regarded as one of the main problems concerning obedience in religious congregations. She answered, "Our main problem is that many of the sisters do not feel personally responsible for the congregation. They are obedient in the traditional sense, i.e., they ask permission, etc., but what is lacking is a real feeling for the group charism and for the responsibility that should flow from it." We all know well how often members start thinking about the congregation's charism only when they find themselves elected provincials or appointed to formation work.

b. In this view of obedience, we have to look at the conflict that may arise between my personal calling and the group charism. I am a unique person with personal charisms, which are not suspended once I accept a group charism. Therefore, I cannot dispense myself from what is called the "discernment of the Holy Spirit" with regard to the work I am asked to undertake within the broad scope of the congregations's charism. I have to discern how my personal charism and the charism of the congregation, which demands of me this or that work, harmonize with each other. Obedience does not mean I necessarily say yes to everything I am asked to do, but demands discernment. My final "yes" will be the result of a free and deliberate choice which I make on the basis of an honest discernment process.

How often I have met religious men and women who have always said "yes, yes" to all they were asked to do, but, at the end of the road are full of bitterness and resentment, since they never REALLY said "yes'" to the assignments they were asked to undertake. Even blind obedience is a virtue only if a decision is gained through discernment. We talk today so much about equality and participation. They, however, must first be applied to ourselves before we demand them of others. Participation means that people have a right to participate in the process that affects their lives.

For contemporary religious the vow of obedience has become an intrinsic element of their prophetic **struggle for liberation and justice.**

What religious can bring to the worldwide struggle against domination is a deep hunger and thirst for justice based on their own spiritual experience of liberation in Jesus Christ. Religious are people who know that justice and holiness are finally identical, and that justice is not merely the way humans can and should relate to each other as brothers and sisters which is given to us by the God who created and redeemed us all.

It might be suggested that religious should be on the cutting edge in the development of new forms of community life and organization structured by and for justice. Here, if anywhere, it makes sense for the members to trust one another and thus to be able to abandon all forms of domination, coercion, intolerance and forced conformity...Religious should offer a prophetic witness that it is possible for a group to live together in love and justice celebrating their own freedom and equality in the very act of celebrating God's absolute and respectful reign in their lives. (Sandra M.Schneider, *New Wineskin*)

c. Obedience, in the context of group charism, demands of the superior and his council a real discernment process in making appointments. Is the work the superiors ask from one of their members in line with the congregation's charism? Is the unique charism of the individual taken into consideration as well? I believe that a superior fails in his or her responsibility towards the group charism if he or she lets a member have his or her own will when the ministry in question is way out of the scope of the congregation or of the group's charism. At times it is easier to let a member have his or her way than to responsibly respect the group charism and say "no" to the individual. All of us know only too well that there is a constant temptation to elect a superior who lets us have our own way, who does not question our work, or disturb our lifestyles, who, in short, "does not rock the boat." Superiors of that kind are in the long run a disaster for the congregation or group.

d. Lastly the vow of obedience demands that the superior decide what work the member should take up. This "giving of the mission" must be accepted by the person concerned as the will of God for him or her, if there are no serious objections to it.

Many spiritual writers point out that nothing erodes the effectivity of a religious community more than the superior's unwillingness to make necessary decisions and so to allow matters to go undecided for years. Responsibility for the group charism demands this kind of obedience from the superior no matter how difficult it may sometimes be.

Summary

In this conference I have tried to explain the vow of obedience in the context of group charism. Although this is not the only approach, it places this vow in the concrete situation of a vocation. After all, the active religious try to live the three vows which are meant to help us follow and imitate more freely and more closely the Lord, as he presents himself in the Gospel.

Today, new groups and communities are emerging in the Church. Their vision is to live the Gospels anew in our age and time. They could as well be "God's new therapy" for his Church and human society" alongside with renewed religious life. They seem to provide the Church and society with much needed new models of discipleship and Christian community living. They might become God's new "contrast society" for today. Existing congregations are expected to go on existing only if they are willing to take the basic new inspirations of these newly-arising groups and incorporate them into their own constitutions. Four distinctive elements mark these emerging communities:

1) They reveal a great confidence in the Holy Spirit. If there is a work to be done they never ask: "Do we have the money? Do we have the personnel?" No, the question is simply, "Does the Holy Spirit want us to do it?"

2) They show a deep sense of responsibility for the spiritual life of each one in the community. They are deeply concerned with the spiritual growth of each member.

3) The members share the personal experiences of their spiritual life: they share Christ. At least, once a week they meet to exchange and share their spiritual life-experiences.

4) The members' experience of Christ is based on a personal conversion and not on theoretical knowledge. For them the "second conversion", which is the actual basis of their faith-sharing, is very important.

Questions for Reflection:

1. What understanding of obedience do I hold?

2. Do I care for my congregation's group charism, its spirituality and its exercise?

3. Which of the above mentioned four elements do you think are worth being considered as essential for your congregation?

Story for Reflection:

INDIFFERENCE

A young minister went to his first church with eager enthusiasm. To his disappointment, he found the worship services poorly attended and the spiritual life of the congregation at low ebb. He called from house to house seeking renewed interest, but several people said the church was so dead that they did not care to attend. He discussed the situation with his church board and they agreed the criticism was probably justified.

The pastor announced that since the church was considered dead, he would conduct its funeral the following Sunday. The church was crowded that day. In front of the pulpit was a coffin. The minister eulogized the deceased. He told how much the church had accomplished in the past and expressed his sorrow over its untimely demise. Then he invited the congregation to go forward and view the corpse. One by one the people looked into the casket; each was amazed to see his own face reflected from a mirror in the bottom of the coffin. Many were shocked and indignant, but then each member began to realize that his or her own spiritual indifference was the reason the church was dead.

(Paul J. Wharton, *Stories and Parables*, p 51)

PRAYER FOR THE GIFT OF OBEDIENCE

Lord Jesus, help me to hear you better and to live in obedience to your loving will for me. Give me a great increase in the charism of obedience according to the spirit of my institute so that I may follow you in the way for which you have chosen me, so that I may not shrink from the cross but carry it in union with you.

Help me, through a new outpouring of the charism of obedience into my heart and my will, to obey your loving will always and to live in the spirit of listening and of readiness to hear your word and do it.

Give me the surrender, that may say yes to you in all things, laying down my life daily for love of you. Give me the grace of being obedient even unto death and to live that same kenosis, that same emptying out, that you lived so that I may be filed with your light and your Spirit. Let me live your "emptying out", Lord in my daily contemplation in humble and loving reverence. Let me live it in my community and in my apostolate in reverent service and in obedience to you in all the ways you speak to me. Let me live it in my death, however you call me to come to you finally.

Amen.

(R. Faricy)

MARY AS THE MODEL OF TRUE DISCIPLESHIP: SHE WALKED BY FAITH AND NOT BY SIGHT

Introduction

The theme of this book has been discipleship. I would like to conclude by presenting to you a "perfect model" of what it means to be a true disciple of Jesus: MARY, THE MOTHER OF OUR LORD.

Jesus' own life was ruled by two principles:

- total dedication to the Father
- total dedication to his mission.

Mary's life was ruled by the same principles:

Total dedication to the Father: "Let it be done according to your will (Lk 1:38).

Total dedication to the mission of her Son, "Do whatever he tells you" (Jn 2:5).

There are three things that distinguish us Catholics from other denominations:

- the Petrine ministry;
- the Eucharist as the central act of worship;
- devotion to Mary.

We have just behind us a century of increased Marian devotion. The years 1854 - 1950 were marked by the Marian dogmas; the Immaculate Conception and the Assumption of Mary. Vatican II tried to put things into perspective and stopped a few excesses. Many wanted a new, separate document on Mary and to climax the development in Mariology through a new dogma: Mediatrix of all graces. But the Council thought otherwise. It did give Mary a new title which is probably the most biblical there is — MOTHER OF THE CHURCH, i.e., the mother of the community of people who have made it their life task to follow Jesus. She is the mother of the disciples of Jesus. With this view the Council went back to the Scriptures.

If we look at the Gospels we discover that interest in Mary was progressing. Mark and Matthew have not much to say about her, but Luke and John have her playing a more decisive role in the life of Jesus and the Church. Not only is she there when the Messiah entered the world but also when the Church is born at Pentecost.

The image of Mary needs a lot of change in our imagination. If we take the Incarnation seriously and if Jesus was the greatest religious leader ever born, his mother must have been a remarkable woman — and not the sweet little girl that disappeared into the background of Jesus' life. The more we take seriously the humanity of Christ, the more his mother moves into the foreground as an extraordinary woman, who not only bore such a man, but who also raised him. It seems that the woman who was so fascinated with Jesus spontaneously realized what a mother he must have had when she exclaimed, "Blessed the womb that bore you and the breasts you sucked" (Lk 11:27).

Luke's Gospel, written around the year 80 A.D., i.e., one generation after her death, reveals a remarkable devotion to Mary already present in the community for which and in which he wrote his Gospel. Around that time we already find a developed devotion to her among some communities.

John, who always sees her in connection with the Church, put her at the opening and closing of Jesus' ministry: at Cana and under the cross (Jn 2:1-11; 19:25-27).

I would like now to present to you the main biblical texts that refer to Mary and to show through these texts what discipleship really implies: TO WALK BY FAITH AND NOT BY SIGHT.

The Annunciation story (Lk 1:26-38)

Here we find all the typical elements of a classic vocation story. It follows the pattern of the way the prophets were called in the Old Testament:

Greeting: "Full of grace, you are a chosen one." Every call is a gift from God and not something one can choose on his or her own.

Reaction to Mary: She was deeply troubled by the angel's message. She was afraid.

God's answer: "Do not be afraid." The mission she has to fulfill contains the promise that she will get the necessary strength to carry it out. There is, therefore, no real reason to fear.

Mary's final answer: She gives her unconditional "YES", which leads her to a jubilant song, her Magnificat.

We should not forget that the reality of such a call needed a strong woman. She was terrified by the extraordinary vocation. Yet her "fiat" comes as a courageous response that took into consideration all the spiritual, physical, psychological, and social consequences which such a "yes" would imply.

Every call is a gracious gift, a charism. Christ chooses whom he wants, "I chose you; you did not choose me" (Mk 3:31). Everyone who has been called has experienced fear and anxiety about his or her vocation. But we should also keep God's assurance in mind, when fear and apprehension arise, "Do not be afraid! I will give you the necessary strength to fulfill your mission." If we then give our unconditional "Yes" to this calling by trusting the Lord's assurance, an inner peace and joy will be ours as well.

This does not mean all difficulties, anxieties and fears will disappear. Many will remain with us forever. But in spite of this there can be an inner peace and joy that enable us to bear everything that comes our way, since we do not have to rely on our own strength but on God's promise and assistance. At times it is good to remember what Paul tells us:

Who then can ever keep Christ's love from us? When we have trouble or calamity, when we are hunted down or destroyed, is it because he doesn't love us anymore?...nothing can ever separate us from his love (Rm 8:35).

There is a similarity between Mary's call and our call. The only difference is the way she answered the call and the way we do.

The birth of Jesus: The test of her faith (Lk 2:1-21)

The birth of Jesus is embarrassingly human according to divine standards. It is contrary to any expectation humans might have had as to how God might enter this world. He came without splendor or glory. Jesus was not born with a halo. All that Mary had was her faith. There were signs that could support her faith: the virginal conception, the shepherds, the wise men from the East. But again, this faith is also put to the test right away. Herod wants to kill the child and they have to flee into exile (Mt 2:13). Whatever was the mystery behind this child? Could God not protect himself?

So, too, things in our religious and priestly lives can be so embarrassingly human that we would like to hide them from outsiders. How often have I thought, and I am sure you have too, that if people knew who I really am, if they knew me with all my weaknesses and faults, what would these people say? Remember all the enthusiasm with which we entered religious life or the seminary, all the heroic resolutions we made? I was sure in the novitiate that I would become a saint. But, "where have all the flowers gone?"

The incarnation of our vocation can be so human. It needs great faith to hold on to the divine dimension in a vocation. It often takes great courage to live this way of life, just to walk by faith and to trust in the divine hidden in all this humanness. But we should not forget that God keeps things in balance. If we search our lives, there are enough signs that prove our commitment is a 'reasonable option'. There are times when we just have to rely on what we once saw.

Martin Heidegger's picture of life may illustrate this point. He compared the journey of life to a person walking in a huge forest, where it is pitch dark, where it is raining and thundering and one has completely lost the way. Suddenly there is a bolt of lightning, and for an instant, the way is clear. Then it is dark again. All one can and must do is to keep going in the direction one saw illuminated by the lightning flash.

Most of our life we must move ahead in darkness, sustained in our faithfulness by that which we once glimpsed when, even if only for an instant, everything was clear. That is exactly what Mary did. When it was dark and she could not understand anymore, she kept to what she had seen, walking by faith not by sight.

The Presentation in the temple (Lk 2:22-37)

The closer she became to the mission of her Son, the more Mary would have to share in his mission. The leading sentence of this story is: "Sorrow, like a sharp sword, will break your heart." Mary must have been shocked by these words. The text tells us: "They did not understand, but Mary kept all this in her heart and pondered over it". She walked by faith and not by sight! However, there is some light given. Simeon and Anna testify to the child. But when they reach home their ordinary life went on. They were a family like any other. This is the mystery of the Incarnation: Jesus became human in everything (Ph 2:7). And if being human meant for Christ that at times he had to cry with tears to his Father (Heb 5:7), can we presume that it was easier for his mother, who shared her Son's mission so intimately?

When we entered religious or priestly life, did we think that life would be as it is now? It takes some time till we come to realize that greatness consists in doing ordinary things in an extraordinary way. When A. Janssen, the founder of the SVD and SSpS religious congregations, was beatified, a cardinal in the beatification celebration asked, "What did this man do that made him a saint?" And his answer was, "This man did the ordinary things in life in an extraordinary way." The same message was communicated to me by a sticker someone once put on my door. It read: "Big shots are little shots who keep on shooting."

The twelve-year-old boy in the temple (Lk 2:41-52)

Mary thought she knew her Son. Yet, once again her faith was tested. What an agony and fear must have gripped Mary and Joseph, knowing as they did that kidnapping was a very common practice during festivals. Children were sold into Egypt as slaves. When his parents finally found Jesus, his answer was seemingly unconcerned, "Why did you look for me?" They did not understand what he was saying. Jesus remained a mystery to them. Yet they had to live with that mystery twenty more years. "And he went back with them to Nazareth, where he was obedient to them." Once again we could say that they lived by faith and not by sight.

We will never understand God's actions completely. Many things will remain dark and hard to accept if we believe that God loves all human beings unconditionally. How often have I asked God, "Why do you do this to me or to my friends, to humankind, to the Church?" No answer. Mary asked her Son, "Why did you do this to us?" and did not get an answer. Neither will we. How often have I thought, "God, you are not fair!"

The story is told that the great Teresa of Avila was on a journey one day and stepped out of her carriage to find herself knee-deep in mud. Disgusted with her situation she supposedly said, "Lord, if you do this to your friends, no wonder you have only a few of them."

Most of the time the only attitude we can take is the one Mary had: "His mother treasured all these things in her heart." What she could not understand she pondered over, knowing that it all must have a meaning in God's love for each of us.

The public life of Jesus (Mk 3:20; 3:13)

For Mary, the public life of Jesus was full of ambiguities. There were the miracles, the mighty works and deeds. But there were also other voices. "When his family heard about all this, they set out to get him because people were saying 'He has gone mad!'" (Mk 3:20). And in the same chapter (v.31), we are informed that the family had arrived with his mother and wanted to talk with him. His relatives wanted to lock him up because he had become a scandal for the family. Their intention was to take him home and save the family from embarrassment. If Joseph was dead, it was the uncle's duty to take charge of the greater family.

Mary, his Mother, had no say in this. What an agony it must have been for her. She must have felt an utter helplessness in not knowing what the relatives were going to do with him, although she was deeply convinced that her Son had a mission. Jesus' answer to the remark that his family is outside waiting for him is a puzzle, "Who are my mother, my brother and my sister?" The one thing that seems to be sure is that Jesus knew well that his mother was a true disciple of his, not just because she was his mother, but because she lived by the same principles that ruled his own life — total dedication to the will of the Father and to his mission.

Jesus' remark shows what counts for him. It makes no difference whether I am a priest, a religious, a bishop or hold any ecclesiastical rank. What really counts is the will of the Father. The rest is unessential. What matters is not how deeply I know and understand who Jesus is, but only my willingness to do what Jesus wants me to do even though I do not grasp the meaning of it all.

Mary under the cross (Jn 19:25-27)

"Mother, there is your son; son, there is your mother."

This is Jesus' last will. The beloved disciple in the gospel of John is always the prototype of all disciples who will come to follow the Lord. The dying Jesus recommends his disciples to the care of his mother. It is as if he is saying, "Mother, you know what it means to be a true disciple of mine. Please, take care of them and make sure they will become what you yourself lived so faithfully." The title Vatican II gave to Mary is exactly what Jesus wanted her to be — the mother of his disciples, that is, the Mother of the Church.

But Jesus also tells the disciple to take care of his mother. This is a theological statement and not just a petition that John should care for Mary since Jesus is gone and no one would care for her. It means the disciple should develop a healthy devotion to Mary, since she, like no one else, can really teach and guide him or her in the most essential task on earth — to become a true disciple of Jesus.

Our Catholic faith has always known and practiced this devotion to Mary as our Mother. Thousands of shrines and Churches have been built in her honor. Numerous congregations and sodalities carry her name. There is no religious order that has not a passage in its constitution which encourages the members to develop a healthy devotion to Mary. If we look at all the apparitions the Catholic Church holds as genuine, they all reveal one basic truth: Mary always proves to be deeply concerned with the community of the disciples of Jesus, the Church. Her real care and intention has always been to make us into true disciples of her Son, to fulfill her Son's last request on earth, "Mother, take care of my disciples." As she was faithful to the mission of her Son up to the last moment, so she will remain faithful to her Son's last will as long as there are people who have decided to enter into fellowship with him.

The Gospels are the 'handbooks', the 'manuals' of discipleship. They present us with different ways of following the Lord. So we cannot say there is only one way. There are many ways, and we should never use the degree of Marian devotion a person professes as a measuring stick for his or her being a true disciple of Jesus.

Without saying, therefore, that one cannot be a true disciple of Jesus without a deep devotion to Mary, we can with certainty say that to have a genuine devotion to Mary, our Mother, is one of the best guarantees of moving in the direction of becoming a true disciple of Jesus. Mary knows perfectly well what a true disciple is, and all the care and help she has always shown to millions of people who have confidently turned to her, have had, in the last analysis, only one aim and goal — to make them better disciples of her Son.

Some years ago on a plane, I met a guru. He had a string of beads which he kept passing through his fingers. I asked him what he was doing. He replied,

"We use these to soothe our nerves." We talked about this in detail, and then he asked me, "Don't you Catholics have something similar?" "Yes", I replied, "but we don't use them to soothe our nerves." Then he told me, "Father, if you want to concentrate on something, you have to have something in your hand that keeps your attention steady."

It seems to me that the rosary is an excellent means to meditate with Mary on the mysteries of our faith and to get to know Christ. She was the true disciple of Jesus who really understood him. When you pray the rosary, it is as if she walks beside you and explains to you the mysteries of our faith in order to make you a truer disciple of Jesus. Her whole concern is that with her help we become true disciples of her Son. Allowing Mary to accompany us in life means to walk as she did: BY FAITH AND NOT BY SIGHT.

Questions for Reflection:

1. Do I draw strength for my life by reflecting on Mary's response to God as revealed in Scripture? Is she a 'flesh and blood' example for me?

2. In my life how have I experienced the call to 'walk by faith and not by sight?

MAGNIFICAT OF ACCEPTANCE:

My soul trembles in the presence of the loving Creator and my spirit prepares itself to walk hand in hand with the God who saves Israel because I have been accepted by God as a simple helpmate.

Yes, forever in the life of humankind people will sing of this loving encounter; through remembering this moment, the faithful will know all things are possible in God. Holy is the place within me where God lives. God's tender fingers reach out from age to age to touch the softened inner spaces of those who open their souls in hope.

I have experienced the creative power of God's embracing arms and I know the cleansing fire of unconditional love.

I am freed from all earthly authority and know my bonding to the Author of all earthly things.

I am filled with the news of good things; my favor with God, faithful trust in the gentle shadow of the most High, the mystery of my son, Jesus, the gift of companionship with my beloved kinswoman, Elizabeth, who believes as I believe. The place in my heart that I had filled with thoughts of fear and inadequacy has been emptied and I am quiet within.

God comes to save Israel, our holy family, remembering that we are the ones who remember, ...according to the kinship we have known... remembering that we are the ones who remember and that where God and people trust each other there is home. (Ann Johnson, *Myriam of Nazareth*)

NINETEENTH CONFERENCE

THE KINGDOM AT WORK IN US: SIGNS OF TRUE DISCIPLESHIP

Introduction

Discipleship is the theme of our retreat: OUR way of following the Lord. In relation to this, a question is often asked: How can I know whether or not the Gospel message of God's Kingdom has really taken root, or is taking root, in me? How do I know that I am truly on the way to fellowship, that Christ has made his home in me? Or to use a more traditional language, how do I know whether or not God's grace is operative in me?

There are some INDICATORS. I do think they can give us an adequate answer to the above questions. I would like to present to you four such indicators. Although there might be more, these four have proven to me to be quite valid in my working with all kinds of people.

1. Am I convinced that God loves me unconditionally the way I am? How far do I live out this conviction?

This is the real test! Bernanos, a French philosopher, once said, "There is no incident in my life so small that I cannot discover behind it God's love and providence for me."

We all know how difficult it is at times to believe that everything that happens to me should be seen as the result of God's will and providence. This might be possible as long as things in my life turn out well, but what about all the negative events which are part of every life, things like accidents, sickness, natural catastrophes? How can I ever assume that behind such things lies God's will, that has only my well-being at heart?

In my own life over the years, I have come to see difficulties and unpleasant things in a more positive way. Whatever might happen to me, whatever job I am assigned to do, whatever mess I might get myself into, whatever failure and weakness I have to face in my life as my own doing, I can always count on one sure reality: GOD'S UNCONDITIONAL LOVE IS RIGHT THERE WITH ME IN THAT SITUATION. Not that he is the one who caused the difficulties, rather, he is there with his love. Therefore, the question is not who or what caused this situation or misfortune. The amazing reality is that his love is right there in order to "PASCHALIZE" this situation, as bad as it may be, and to make out of this stumbling block a stepping stone for a better future. The famous SONG OF LOVE in 1 Co 13:4-8 is first of all God's own love song.

> Love is patient and kind. It does not insist on its own way; it is not irritable or resentful...; it bears all things, it never gives up, believes all things, hopes all things, endures all things (1 Co 13:4).

> For I know the plans I have for you, says the Lord, plans for your welfare not for your woe, to give you a future full of hope (Jr 29:11).

> How could I part with you, how could I give you up? My heart recoils from it; my whole being trembles at the thought (Ho 11:8).

> Even if a mother forgets her baby, the fruit of her womb, I will never forget you my people (Is 49:19).

I must come to realize how God's love has dogged my steps from the beginning, how it has not given up on me, how God seeks and loves me in spite of myself. This asks at times for deep faith, yet one has to take time out to search through one's life and then one will discover God's love all the way through. The opposite of love is, as I have previously emphasized, not hatred, but indifference. Sin is, therefore, my indifference to God's unconditional love for me, which I might consider now and again as a nice thought but which I could hardly say permeates my life.

Accepting God's unconditional love does not mean that many things and events in my life that remain dark, troublesome and puzzling will be resolved. Whole areas in me are still unredeemed and sin-permeated. However, with such a view of God's love, I can bear this with a compassionate love for myself - in the same way as Christ bears my unredeemedness and sin-permeatedness without giving up on me.

> In our world of loneliness and despair, there is an enormous need for men and women who know the heart of God, a heart that forgives, that cares, that reaches out and wants to heal. In that heart there is no suspicion, no

vindictiveness, no resentment, and not a tinge of hatred. It is a heart that wants only to give love and to receive love in response. It is a heart that suffers immensely because it sees the magnitude of human pain and the great resistance to trusting the heart of God who wants to offer consolation and hope. (H. Nouwen, *In the Name of Jesus*)

My response to this first question should be then to ask myself and reflect upon the further question: Has the knowledge of God's unconditional love for me as I am now travelled from my head into my heart?

2.Do I recognize that the main problems in my life come from within myself? Do I know how to turn to Christ for healing?

The accent here is on MAIN problems. It is not people, my superiors, the bishop, the weather, circumstances, bad genes, my parents, my surroundings, or any other object, which are the main causes of my problems; rather, it is I myself and all that is happening in me. Some people manage to blame everyone and everything in their lives except themselves for any problem they have.

> Listen to me, all of you, and understand. There is nothing that goes into a person form the outside which can make him unclean. Rather, it is what comes out of the person that makes him unclean. Listen then, if you have ears to hear with! (Mk 7:18-20)

> God expects but one thing of you, and that is that you should come out of your Self in so far as you are a created being, and let God be God in you. (Meister Eckhart)

Just as important is the realization as to where I can find healing and to whom I should turn for it; that is, to the Lord. The following experience gave me an insight into the healing power of Christ.

A very sociable and intelligent young seminarian was deeply disturbed by an obsession that he was possessed by all kinds of evil power. Things became so bad and he became so violent that it was next to impossible for anyone to live with him. We sought help from psychologists. They advised us to put him into an institution. But we continued praying with him and over him, and this seemed to have the some healing effect. Then one night, he lost control of himself completely. He howled like a dog and shouted so loudly that everyone became deadly afraid to remain in his presence. But stranger still, when morning came this same seminarian came to me and said, "Father John, it is all over, I am healed. Last night, I saw the Lord. He put his hand on me and looked at me with such love that I will never, ever forget this look. At that moment I knew I was healed."

Whatever you may think of this explanation, the seminarian was in fact healed. He never had a recurrence of these attacks again. He is a happy person and a deeply religious man. If you want to hear anyone speak convincingly about the healing power of God's unconditional love, you have to listen to him.

Normally, it is a deep spiritual life, prayer, discernment (alone, and at times with a director), that can lead me to real self-knowledge, and this in turn will bring me to that place where I can receive healing. Nevertheless, this does not mean that such outside forces mentioned above cannot create a lot of real problems. However, if I get the MAIN problem, i.e., MYSELF, really under control, I can live relatively peacefully with all kinds of problems. With a compassionate love I can even help to redeem them.

3. Do I love with a Christ-like love? Am I growing in understanding, in compassion and tolerance towards the people with whom I have to live?

A new commandment I give you; love one another. As I have loved you, so you must love one another. If you have love for one another, then all will know that you are my disciples (Jn 13: 34-35).

The Lord does not just ask us to love each other in general terms. He specifies the disciples' love by saying that we must love each other "AS HE" has loved us. This "as I have loved you" becomes the determining factor of any Christian love. But how did Christ love us? What kind of love does he demand?

Christ's love is firstly, a UNIVERSAL love, and secondly, it is COMPASSIONATE. UNIVERSAL means he loved all, but especially the poor, the marginalized, the outcast, those, that the so-called respectable people would have nothing to do with (Mt 5:44-47).

How can one learn to love as Christ did?

The only way is to follow the Lord and to learn from him by doing. There is no other way.

First, one has to contemplate Christ as the Gospels portray him; to contemplate what he said, what he did, to study lovingly his mind, his heart, his way of thinking, his way of seeing things, his relation to the Father, his relation to his fellow human beings. This is what it means to be a Christian — to have Christ at the very center of one's life as the measure of one's humanity, to learn from him, to put on his mind and heart, to become more and more like him. Gradually, in this way, I will start loving as he loved. What is at the heart of the Gospel is not an idea, not even an idea as sublime as that of love, but a person — Jesus Christ. God and man, the very incarnation of God's love.

Second, if you really want to know whether you love as Christ loved us, there is a kind of indicator of where you stand: Do I love only those who love me or do I also love those who are, humanly speaking, less lovable, who go against the grain, who contradict me, frustrate me? We all know how easy it is to love some and how difficult it is to love others. But if we look at Jesus, we see that he loved everyone, especially the less lovable. Our love, too, must reach out to those who need it most. Attractive persons do not need our love in any special way, for they are loved by all. Dull personalities, those who are troubled, or, in extreme cases, those who are downright selfish, turned in on themselves, need love and need it desperately.

Wherever we are we will find that there are three groups of people we have to work with:

1. There is a small group made up of those we get along with extremely well. We click with them, we like them and they like us. These are our friends.

2. At the other end of the gamut, we find a small group of those who somehow or other just grate on us, who go against the grain.

3. Then there is that much larger group in between the other two. It consists of those who greet us and whom we greet. We do what we have to do for them, but it does not go beyond that.

The small group of friends at the one end is very important for us. It is there that we see what love draws us to do, what love between human persons consists of. We greet them with a smile. For them we have time. If they make a mistake we can overlook it. But, what we do for this small group of friends we have to be able to do, when the occasion calls for it, for that larger group in the middle and even for the smaller group at the other end.

It is not that we have to love everyone equally. Even Jesus had people he called friends and a favorite family. But our love for our friends should not close us off from others; rather, it should help us open ourselves up to all. Jesus' love is an 'inclusive' love as well as a compassionate love, a love that embraces all and suffers with, that bears and understands, that stays with us in whatever kind of situations we might find ourselves.

Therefore, the real measure of my growth in the Spirit is my genuine concern, kindness, understanding, tolerance and compassion towards people with whom I have to live. Do I bear with them and even myself the way Christ bears with me and them - with COMPASSION? Can I say that it is compassion that guides my work with people? Or do rules and regulations, like Canon Law, determine my ministry? Am I like Linus, who said, "I love humankind, it is people I cannot stand."

Therese of Lisieux describes one of her deepest insights concerning her love for others with these words:

> I understand now that charity consists in bearing with the faults of others, in not being surprised at their weakness, in being edified by the smallest act of virtue we see them practice. (P.O'Connor, *Therese of Lisieux*)

All that doesn't mean that I will never get upset or angry anymore, that nothing can disturb me. We remain human as long as we live, and the greatest act of compassion might be that which we have to show towards ourselves — in the way Christ loves us and bears with us.

This third point is really THE rule of thumb by which to measure whether or not the Kingdom of God has taken root in us.

> Wisdom begins when one at last experiences that the ultimate charism is love. Only love reveals the truth within another person. Man's greatest achievement lies not in art, nor in science, politics, economics but in the realm of human friendship. There is no other human power. Friendship does not rest on education, talent, inheritance but solely in the human heart. (E. Farrell, *Disciples And Other Strangers*)

True friendship

Time before time, when the world was young, two brothers shared a field and a mill, each night dividing evenly the grain they had ground together during the day. One brother lived alone; the other had a wife and a large family. Now the single brother thought to himself one day, "It isn't really fair that we divide the grain evenly. I have only myself to care for, but my brother has children to feed." So each night he secretly took some of his grain to his brother's granary to see that he was never without.

But the married brother said to himself one day, "It isn't really fair that we divide the grain evenly, because I have children to provide for me in my old age, but my brother has no one. What will he do when he's old?" So every night he secretly took some of his grain to his brother's granary. As a result, both of them always found their supply of grain mysteriously replenished each morning.

Then one night as they met each other halfway between their two houses, they suddenly realized what had been happening, and they embraced each other in love. The story is that God witnessed their meeting and proclaimed, "This is a holy place - a place of love - and here it is that my temple shall be built." And so it was. The holy place where God is made known to...people, is the place where human beings discover each other in love. (W. Bausch, *Storytelling*)

4. Is my life permeated by a permanent joy and peace?

If we live out of the knowledge of God's unconditional love for us, a deep peace and joy will pervade our entire life. This again does not mean that we will never experience disturbances and turmoil at times, but that, when we do, we can retain a calmness that originates from our Christian faith. If there is anything the world needs today, it is people who radiate the joy of a redeemed life. We have so many doomsday preachers all around us - but who is telling us the GOOD NEWS of the kingdom? F. Nietzsche once said, "I could believe in a redeemer, if his followers looked more redeemed." So often in his epistles Paul urges us to radiate our joy over God's redeeming presence in our lives:

Speak to one another in the words of psalms, hymns and sacred songs, sing hymns and psalms to the Lord with praise in your heart. Always give thanks for everything to God the Father, in the name of our Lord Jesus Christ (Ep 5:19-20).

May you always be joyful in your life in the Lord. I say it again: rejoice! (Ph 4:4).

In conclusion, my brothers and sisters, fill your minds with those things that are good and deserve praise: things that are true, noble, right, pure and lovely, and honorable (Ph 4:8).

Sing psalms, hymns, and sacred songs; sing to God with thanksgiving in your hearts. Everything you do or say then should be done in the name of the Lord Jesus, as you give thanks through him to God the Father (Col 3:16-17).

Some spiritual writers have insisted that we need today a special kind of fasting: MIND-FASTING. This means we should not allow depressing, destructive and negative thoughts to enter our minds. This really demands a discipline, a fasting. Instead of negative thoughts, we should do what St. Paul suggests: SPIRIT-FEASTING, i.e., we should fill our minds and hearts with all the noble and joyful things the Gospel speaks of and in so doing really communicate to people what they need to hear from us. (B.J. Tyrell, *Christotherapy: Healing Through Enlightenment*)

I would like to conclude with a quote from "Evangelii Nuntiandi":

And may the world of our time, which is searching with anguish, sometimes with hope, be enabled to receive the Good News not from evangelizers who are dejected, discouraged, impatient or anxious, but ministers of the Gospel whose lives glow with fervor, who have received the joy of Christ. (par 80)

Questions for Reflection:

1. How convinced am I that God loves me as I am now? Do I live out of this knowledge?

2. Whom or what do I blame for my problems in life? Am I eager to ask Christ to heal what needs healing in my life?

3. What guides my relationship with the people with whom I have to live day in, day out? Am I a compassionate person or a judging person? Do I exclude certain persons from my love?

4. Can I say that an inner joy and peace underlies my life, and is it something I can return to again and again?

THE RABBI'S GIFT

There was a famous monastery which had fallen on very hard times. Formerly its many buildings were filled with young monks and its big church resounded with the singing of the chant, but now it was deserted. People no longer came there to be nourished by prayer. A handful of old monks shuffled through the cloisters and praised their God with heavy hearts.

On the edge of the monastery woods, an old rabbi had built a little hut. He would come there from time to time to fast and pray. No one ever spoke with him, but whenever he appeared, the word would be passed from monk to monk, "The rabbi walks in the woods." And, for as long as he was there, the monks would feel sustained by his prayerful presence.

One day the abbot decided to visit the rabbi and to open his heart to him. So, after the morning Eucharist, he set out through the woods. As he approached the hut, the abbot saw the rabbi standing in the doorway, his arms outstretched in welcome. It was as though he had been waiting there for some time. The two embraced like long-lost brothers. Then they stepped back and just stood there, smiling at one another with smiles their faces could hardly contain.

After a while the rabbi motioned the abbot to enter. In the middle of the room was a wooden table with the Scriptures open on it. They sat there for a moment, in the presence of the book. Then the rabbi began to cry. The abbot could not contain himself. He covered his face with his hands and began to cry too. For the first time in his life, he cried his heart out. The two men sat there like lost children, filling the hut with their sobs and wetting the wood of the table with their tears.

After the tears had ceased to flow and all was quiet again, the rabbi lifted his head. "You and your brothers are serving God with heavy hearts," he said. "You have come to ask a teaching of me. I will give you a teaching, but you can only repeat it once. After that, no one must ever say it aloud again."

The rabbi looked straight at the abbot and said,"The Messiah is among you."

For a while, all was silent. Then the rabbi said, "Now you must go."

The abbot left without a word and without ever looking back.

The next morning, the abbot called his monks together in the chapter room. He told them he had received a teaching from "the rabbi who walks in the woods" and that this teaching was never to be spoken aloud. Then he looked at each of his brothers and said, "The rabbi said that one of us is the Messiah."

The monks were startled by this saying. "What could it mean?" they asked themselves. "Is Brother John the Messiah? Or Father Matthew? Or Brother Thomas? Am I the Messiah? What could this mean?"

They were all deeply puzzled by the rabbi's teaching. But no one ever mentioned it again.

As time went by, the monks began to treat one another with a very special reverence. There was a gentle, wholehearted, human quality about them now which was hard to describe but easy to notice. They lived with one another as men who had finally found something. But they prayed the Scriptures together as men who were always looking for something. Occasional visitors found themselves deeply moved by the lives of these monks. Before long, people were coming from far and wide to be nourished by the prayer life of the monks and young men were asking, once again, to become part of the community.

In those days, the rabbi no longer walked in the woods. His hut had fallen into ruins. But, somehow or other, the old monks who had taken his teaching to heart still felt sustained by his prayerful presence.

(William J. Bausch, *Storytelling*, Imagination and Faith, pp 138-140)

SELECTED BIBLIOGRAPHY

Wilkie Au, *By Way of the Heart, Towards a Holistic Christian Spirituality*, Geoffrey Chapman: London 1990.

Leslie F. Brandt, *Psalms Now*, Concordia Publishing House: St. Louis, Missuri, 1973.

Ruth Burrows, *To Believe in Jesus*, Sheed and Ward: London, 1978.

Martin Buber, *Erzählungen der Chassidim*, Manesse Verlag: Zuerich, 1990.

William J. Bausch, *Storytelling*, Twenty-Third Publications, Mystic, Connecticut, 1991.

Walter Brueggemann, Sharon Parks, Thoams H. Groome, *To Act Justly, Love Tenderly, Walk Humbly" An Agenda for Ministers*, Paulist Press: New York, 1986

Charles Elliott, *Praying the KingdomTowards a Political Spirituality*, Darton, Longman and Todd: London, 1985.

Robert Faricy, *The End of the Religious Life*, Winston Press, 1983

Edward Farrell, *Free to be Nothing*, Dominican Publications: Dublin, 1989.

Edward Farrell, *Disciples And Other Strangers*, Dimension: Denville, N.Y., 1974.

David A. Fleming, S.M. *Pilgrim's Notebook*, Orbis: New York, 1992.

C. Futrell, "The Challenge of Ministry" in *Human Development 2* (1982) pp 87-93, Compossed by Sr. Charity.

Segundo Galilea, *Following Jesus*, Orbis: New York, 1981.

G. R Grosh, "Models of Poverty" *Review for Religious*, 34 (1974/5) pp. 551-558.

P. Jacobi, *Damit unser Leben gelingen kann*, Matthias Gruenewald-Verlag: Mainz, 1990.

Joachim Jeremias, *Parables of Jesus* , SCM Press: London 1963.

Joachim Jeremias, *Prayers of Jesus*, SCM Press: London, 1967

Ann Johnson, *Myriam of Nazareth*, Notre Dame Indiana: Ave Maria Press, 1984.

John M. Lozano, *Life as Parable*, Reinterpreting The Religious Life, Claretian Publications: Quezon City, Philippines, 1986.

Gerhard Lohfink, "Religious Orders: God's Therapy for the Church", *Theology Digest* 33, (1986), pp. 203-212.

Norbert F. Lohfink, *Option for the Poor*, BIBAL Press: Berkeley, California, 1987.

Carlo M. Martini, *The Testimony of St Paul*, St. Paul Publication: New York, 1981.

Carlo M. Martini, *What am I that you care for me?*, Praying with the psalms, St. Paul Publications, Middlegreen, SLough SL3 6BT: United Kingdom, 1990.

Anthony De Mello, *The Song of the Bird*, Gujarat Sahitya Prakash: Anand, India, 1983.

Anthony de Mello, *One Minute Wisdom*,Gujarat Sahitya Prakash: Anand, India, 1985.

Anthony de Mello, *The Prayer of the Frog*, Vol I, Gujarat Sahitya Prakash: Anand, India, 1988.

L. Morris, *Testament of Love: A Study of Love in the Bible*, Grand Rapids, Michigan: W.B. Erdmans Publishing Company, 1981.

Thomas Merton, *The New Man*, Straus & Cudahy: New York, 1961.

Johannes B. Metz, *Followers of Christ: Religious Life and the Church,* Paulist Press: New York, 1978.

Johannes B.Metz, *Poverty of Spirit*, Newman Press: New York, 1968.

Francis J. Moloney, *Disciples and Prophets, A Biblical Model for the Religious Life*, Darton, Longman and Todd: London, 1980.

Francis J. Moloney, *Free To Love: Poverty, Chastity, Obedience*, Darton, Longman and Todd: London, 1981.

Albert Nolan, *Option for the Poor*, unpublished manuscript.

Henri J.M. Nouwen, *With Open Hands*, Ave Maria Press: Notre Dame, Indiana, 1972

Henri J.M. Nouwen *In the Name of Jesus*, Crossroad: New York, 1989

Henri J.M. Nouwen *Out of Solitude*, Ave Maria Press: Notre Dame, Indiana, 1974.

Henri J.M. Nouwen, Donald P. McNeill, Douglas A. Morrison *Compassion*, Darton, Longman and Todd: London, 1982.

Henri J.M. Nouwen, *Clowning in Rome*, Image Books: New York, 1979

John Shea, *Stories of God*, Thomas More Press: Chicago, 1978.

Sandra M. Schneiders, *New Wineskins: Re-imaging Religious Life Today*, Paulist Press: New York/Mahwah, 1986.

B.J. Tyrell, *Christotherapy: Healing Through Enlightenment*, Seabury Press: New York, 1975.

Paul J. Wharton, *Stories and Parables*, Paulist Press: New York, 1986.

William R. White, *Stories for the Journey A Sourcebook for Christian Storytellers*, Augsburg Publishing House: Minneapolis, 1988.

Eli Wiesel, *Night*, Avon Books: New York, 1969.